To my late father, Mr. K K Ravi,
a man of few words, yet deeply profound. Your quiet strength and timeless wisdom laid the foundation of my character and guided my path. You taught me that true leadership lies in humility, integrity, and resilience. The values you instilled in me have shaped my journey and continue to inspire me every day. Though you are no longer here, your presence and teachings live on in every step I take. This book is a humble tribute to the profound impact you had on my life and the principles you embodied.

REIMAGINING LEADERSHIP IN HIGHER EDUCATION

DIGITAL PATHWAYS TO INSTITUTIONAL EXCELLENCE

ANISH K RAVI

Contents

Contents

Preface

In an era defined by rapid technological advancement and digital innovation, the landscape of higher education is undergoing a seismic shift. Institutions around the world are grappling with challenges and opportunities that require a complete reimagining of leadership, governance, and educational practices. The question is no longer whether higher education should evolve, but how it should navigate this complex transformation to ensure institutional excellence and sustainability in the digital age.

"Reimagining Leadership in Higher Education: Digital Pathways to Institutional Excellence" seeks to address this critical question. This book is a comprehensive exploration of the key aspects of digital transformation in higher education, providing a roadmap for educational leaders, administrators, policymakers, and educators who are at the forefront of this change. Across 25 chapters, it delves into the foundational elements of digital leadership, the practicalities of implementing digital tools and strategies, the ethical considerations in the digital realm, and the future trajectories of higher education in a globalized, interconnected world.

The journey begins with **Chapter 1: The Digital Revolution in Education**, where we set the stage for understanding the profound impact of technology on learning and leadership. The chapter provides a historical context for digital transformation in education, tracing the shift from traditional models to technology-driven paradigms. It highlights how the integration of digital tools—such as learning management systems, artificial intelligence, and virtual reality—has redefined the educational experience, creating new opportunities and challenges for leaders. This chapter serves as a foundation for the book, emphasizing the urgency for leaders to adapt and innovate in a rapidly evolving environment.

Building on this foundation, **Chapter 2: Digital Leadership in the Age of Transformation** explores the essential skills and mindset shifts required for effective educational leadership today. It challenges the traditional notions of leadership and introduces the concept of digital leadership—an approach characterized by agility, inclusivity, and a deep understanding of technology's role in education. The chapter underscores the need for leaders who can not only manage change but also inspire innovation, foster collaboration, and build resilient digital cultures within their institutions.

Recognizing that vision without strategy is merely a dream, **Chapter 3: Strategic Vision and Agile Planning for Digital Transformation** provides a roadmap for crafting and executing forward-thinking strategies in education. This chapter guides readers through the process of setting a clear digital vision, aligning it with institutional goals, and developing agile plans that can adapt to changing circumstances. It highlights the importance of strategic foresight, scenario planning, and stakeholder engagement in successfully navigating digital transformation.

With a strategy in place, the next challenge is implementation, which often involves navigating resistance and managing change. **Chapter 4: Change Management in Digital Education** focuses on leading institutional transformation and overcoming resistance. The chapter offers practical insights into the psychology of change, strategies for building buy-in, and frameworks for managing the complexities associated with digital initiatives. It emphasizes that successful change management is less about technology and more about people—cultivating a culture that embraces innovation and continuous improvement.

As we move deeper into the practicalities of digital transformation, **Chapter 5: Innovative Teaching Models in the Digital Age** explores blended, hybrid, and emerging pedagogical approaches that are redefining teaching and learning. This chapter examines how institutions can leverage technology to create more engaging, flexible, and effective learning experiences. From flipped classrooms to competency-based education, it presents a range of models that cater to diverse learning styles and needs, providing educators with a toolkit to innovate their teaching practices.

Student engagement and motivation are critical to the success of any educational initiative. **Chapter 6: Engagement and Motivation in Digital Learning** delves into the potential of gamification and interactive tools to enhance learning. The chapter highlights innovative strategies that use game design elements, digital storytelling, and interactive simulations to foster a more engaging learning environment. It discusses the psychological principles behind these approaches and provides case studies of institutions that have successfully integrated them into their curricula.

Digital transformation is impossible without a robust technological infrastructure. **Chapter 7: Building the Digital Foundation** discusses the importance of establishing a strong technological backbone for modern educational institutions. This chapter outlines best practices for integrating digital tools and systems, managing IT resources, and ensuring data security. It emphasizes that digital infrastructure is not just about technology but also about creating an environment where technology enhances the educational mission.

While digital transformation offers immense potential, it also risks widening the gap between those with access to digital resources and those without. **Chapter 8: Digital Equity and Inclusion** examines the importance of ensuring that all students and educators have access to digital tools and resources. The chapter explores various initiatives aimed at promoting digital equity in diverse educational contexts, from providing affordable access to technology to designing inclusive digital learning experiences.

In the digital age, data is an invaluable asset for educational leaders. **Chapter 9: Data-Driven Decision Making in Education** analyzes how data analytics is transforming decision-making processes in educational leadership. The chapter discusses the use of data to track student performance, allocate resources, and inform strategic planning. It presents a range of tools and methodologies for leveraging data to drive institutional success and continuous improvement.

As education evolves, so must the educators. **Chapter 10: Professional Development for Digital Competence** focuses on the need for continuous professional development in digital skills for educators. The chapter provides examples of effective training programs that have enhanced teaching quality and discusses the impact of professional development on faculty engagement and student outcomes.

With increased digital integration comes the heightened risk of data breaches and cyber threats. **Chapter 11: Cybersecurity and Data Privacy in Education** explores the challenges of protecting sensitive data in educational institutions. It discusses strategies for implementing robust cybersecurity measures and ensuring data privacy, offering a framework for educational leaders to build a secure digital environment.

The global shift towards online education has been one of the most significant outcomes of the digital revolution. **Chapter 12: E-Learning and Distance Education** examines the rise of e-learning and distance education, focusing on the challenges and opportunities these modalities present for educational leaders. It highlights best practices for designing, delivering, and evaluating online education programs that meet diverse learner needs.

The COVID-19 pandemic has profoundly reshaped educational leadership. **Chapter 13: Leadership in Times of Crisis** reflects on the key lessons learned and strategies for leading institutions through crises. The chapter discusses how leaders can build resilience, maintain continuity, and turn challenges into opportunities for innovation and growth.

In a globalized world, education is a shared endeavor. **Chapter 14: Global Trends in Education** discusses global trends, including the impact of globalization, international collaboration, and the role of educational leaders in navigating these changes. It underscores the importance of cross-border partnerships, cultural competence, and a global mindset in fostering inclusive and forward-looking educational environments.

Innovation is at the heart of digital transformation. **Chapter 15: Building a Culture of Innovation** in Educational Institutions explores how educational leaders can foster a culture of innovation, encouraging experimentation and the adoption of new technologies and methodologies. The chapter provides strategies for nurturing creative thinking and creating an environment where innovation thrives.

Artificial Intelligence (AI) is transforming every aspect of society, and education is no exception. **Chapter 16: The Role of Artificial Intelligence in Education** analyzes the potential of AI to revolutionize education. It presents case studies on AI applications in teaching, administration, and personalized learning, providing insights into how AI can be harnessed to enhance educational outcomes.

Student-centered leadership is essential for digital transformation. **Chapter 17: Student-Centered Leadership in the Digital Age** discusses the importance of focusing on students, using digital tools to enhance engagement, support, and success. The chapter emphasizes that technology should empower students, not replace the human touch in education.

To prepare students for the future, curricula must evolve. **Chapter 18: Curriculum Design for the Future** explores how curricula need to integrate digital literacy, critical thinking, and interdisciplinary studies to meet the demands of the digital age. The chapter provides practical frameworks for designing curricula that are relevant, engaging, and future-focused.

Digital transformation brings ethical challenges. **Chapter 19: Ethics and Digital Responsibility in Education** examines issues such as digital citizenship, online behavior, and the responsibilities of educational leaders. The chapter emphasizes the need for a balanced approach that harnesses the power of technology while safeguarding ethical standards.

EdTech companies are shaping the future of education. **Chapter 20: The Role of EdTech Companies in Shaping the Future of Education** analyzes the influence of these companies on the education sector, including partnerships, innovations, and the implications for educational leadership. The chapter provides insights into how institutions can effectively collaborate with EdTech firms.

Sometimes, the best lessons come from real-world examples. **Chapter 21: Leading Educational Change** presents case studies of successful educational change initiatives from various countries. It highlights the role of leadership in driving these transformations, offering inspiration and practical lessons for educational leaders.

Education must be aligned with the needs of the future workforce. **Chapter 22: Future-Ready Skills and Competencies** discusses the skills and competencies that students need to thrive in the future workforce. The chapter provides a roadmap for educational leaders to ensure their institutions are preparing students for success in an evolving job market.

Governance and policy are critical to the success of digital transformation. **Chapter 23: Governance and Policy in the Digital Age** explores the changing landscape of educational governance and policy, including the challenges and opportunities for educational leaders. The chapter emphasizes the need for adaptive governance models that can respond to the fast-paced changes of the digital age.

As the world grapples with environmental challenges, sustainability is becoming a core mission for educational institutions. **Chapter 24: Sustainability and Education** examines how institutions can lead in promoting sustainable practices and preparing students for a sustainable future. The chapter provides a framework for integrating sustainability into every aspect of institutional strategy and operations.

Finally, **Chapter 25: The Future of Higher Education** offers a forward-looking perspective on the future of higher education. It discusses emerging trends, potential challenges, and the evolving role of educational leadership in the digital age. The chapter calls on educational leaders to embrace change, innovate boldly, and lead with a vision that inspires and transforms.

As you embark on this journey, I encourage you to think critically, reflect deeply, and apply the insights to your own context. The future of higher education is in your hands. By reimagining leadership, embracing digital pathways, and committing to institutional excellence, you can lead the way in creating an education system that is more inclusive, innovative, and impactful for generations to come.

Acknowledgements

First and foremost, I want to thank the Lord Almighty. Without His guidance, grace, and unwavering presence in my life, none of this would have been possible. His strength has carried me through every challenge, and His wisdom has illuminated my path.

I also want to extend my deepest gratitude to everyone who has ever spoken a kind word to me, offered encouragement, or shared a lesson—whether in passing or with intention. I heard it all, and it meant more than you could ever know. Each word, each gesture, has been a thread in the fabric of my journey, shaping me into who I am today.

To my family, friends, mentors, colleagues, and students—thank you for your belief in me, for challenging me to grow, and for being part of this incredible journey. Your support has been my anchor and my inspiration. This book is as much a reflection of your influence as it is of my own thoughts and efforts.

Lastly, to all who have faced their own battles and found the courage to rise above them, this book is for you. May we continue to inspire, uplift, and support one another in our shared quest for knowledge, understanding, and purpose.

The Digital Revolution in Education

"Education is the most powerful weapon which you can use to change the world. — Nelson Mandela"

Think back to a classroom from just a few decades ago—chalkboards, textbooks, and a teacher at the front of the room delivering a lecture. Now, fast forward to today, and that same classroom might look completely different. Students could be sitting with laptops or tablets, engaging with digital content, participating in online discussions, or even attending class virtually from their homes. This is the new reality of education, driven by the digital revolution that has transformed nearly every aspect of how we learn and teach.

The pace of change in education has been nothing short of extraordinary. Technology has opened doors to new ways of learning, making education more accessible and flexible. But with these opportunities come challenges, and the role of leadership in navigating this digital transformation has never been more crucial. In this chapter, we'll explore how the digital revolution is reshaping education, the obstacles that come with it, and the critical role leaders play in guiding their institutions through these changes.

The Digital Shift

Not long ago, education was largely confined to physical classrooms, with teachers delivering lectures and students taking notes. It was a system that worked well for many years, but it had its limitations. Today, digital technology has broken down the walls of the classroom, creating learning environments that are more dynamic, interactive, and inclusive.

Take India's National Education Policy (NEP) 2020, for example. This policy is a bold step towards integrating technology into education across the country. It's not just about bringing in digital tools—it's about rethinking how education is delivered. The NEP 2020 aims to make learning more accessible and inclusive by leveraging technology to reach even the most remote corners of the country. One of its key initiatives is the National Educational Technology Forum (NETF), which fosters collaboration and innovation in using technology to enhance education. Prime Minister Narendra Modi aptly described the NEP 2020 as a transformative initiative, saying, "The NEP 2020 is not just about reforming education, but about transforming it, making it more inclusive, equitable, and rooted in Indian culture, yet aligned with the global technological advancements." This vision underscores how technology isn't just an add-on; it's becoming central to the way education is conceived and delivered.

India's approach highlights how digital transformation in education requires more than just tools—it demands a strategic vision that recognizes the broader societal impacts and strives to bridge the digital divide.

Expanding Access to Education Through Technology

One of the most profound impacts of the digital revolution is its ability to expand access to education. Traditional models of education often left many behind—those who couldn't afford tuition, who lived too far from schools, or who needed to work while studying. Digital technology is changing that, making education more accessible to people from all walks of life.

Consider the explosion of e-learning across Africa. With a young population eager to learn and a shortage of physical educational infrastructure, digital platforms have stepped in to fill the gap. One such platform, Eneza Education, has made a significant impact by providing mobile-based learning in Kenya, Ghana, and Tanzania. What makes Eneza stand out is its accessibility—it works on simple mobile phones, which are widely used even in remote areas with limited internet access. Eneza's approach has reached millions of learners, offering educational content that is not only relevant but also tailored to the needs of students who might otherwise be left out of the formal education system. By allowing students to learn at their own pace and on their own terms, platforms like Eneza are democratizing education in a way that was unimaginable just a few years ago.

The rise of e-learning in Africa is a powerful example of how technology can overcome traditional barriers to education, providing opportunities to those who need them most.

Bridging the Digital Divide

However, the digital revolution isn't without its challenges. The digital divide—the gap between those who have access to digital technologies and those who don't—remains a significant hurdle. This divide isn't just about access to devices or the internet; it's also about digital literacy and the ability to effectively use technology for learning.

In China, the digital divide is particularly evident in rural areas, where internet access and digital literacy are often limited. During the COVID-19 pandemic, this divide became even more apparent as schools across the country shifted to online learning. While students in urban areas adapted quickly, many in rural China were left struggling to keep up. To address this, the Chinese government launched the "Internet Plus Education" program, aiming to connect all rural schools to the internet and provide teachers with the training they need to use digital tools effectively. This initiative goes beyond just providing access—it's about empowering educators and students to make the most of the technology available to them.

China's efforts highlight the complexity of bridging the digital divide. It's not just a matter of installing infrastructure; it's about creating an ecosystem where technology can be used effectively to enhance learning for everyone, regardless of where they live.

The Evolving Role of Educators

As technology reshapes the educational landscape, the role of educators is also changing. Teachers are no longer just transmitters of knowledge—they are becoming facilitators of learning, guiding students as they navigate a world of information that is more vast and complex than ever before.

Finland, renowned for its high-performing education system, has been at the forefront of preparing educators for the digital age. The Finnish National Agency for Education has developed a comprehensive training program that equips teachers with the skills they need to integrate technology into their classrooms effectively. This program focuses on digital pedagogy, helping teachers create interactive content, use digital platforms, and assess student learning in innovative ways. But what makes Finland's approach particularly effective is its emphasis on continuous professional development. Teachers are encouraged to keep learning, to share best practices with their peers, and to experiment with new teaching methods. This culture of continuous improvement ensures that educators remain at the cutting edge of digital teaching. Olli-Pekka Heinonen, the Director General of the Finnish National Agency for Education, summed it up well: "In the digital age, the role of the teacher is more important than ever. Technology can enhance learning, but it is the teacher who brings it to life, guiding students in their journey and helping them to develop the critical thinking skills they need to thrive in a digital world."

Finland's commitment to teacher training underscores the importance of investing in educators as part of the broader digital transformation in education. By equipping teachers with the right tools and skills, we can ensure that technology enhances learning rather than detracts from it.

Leadership in the Digital Revolution

Successfully navigating the digital revolution in education requires strong leadership. Leaders in education must be able to see the big picture, anticipate the challenges that come with digital transformation, and inspire their teams to embrace new ways of teaching and learning.

Singapore is a standout example of how effective leadership can drive digital transformation in education. The country's Smart Nation initiative, launched in 2014, is a comprehensive effort to integrate technology into all aspects of life, including education. As part of this initiative, the Ministry of Education has implemented a digital education strategy that includes deploying digital resources, building digital literacy among students, and integrating technology into the curriculum. Singapore's success can be attributed to strong leadership at both the government and school levels. School leaders are given the autonomy to innovate while being held accountable for their results, creating an environment where experimentation is encouraged, and best practices are shared. This balance of autonomy and accountability has been key to fostering a culture of continuous improvement and innovation in education. As Singapore's Minister for Education, Chan Chun Sing, noted, "In a world where technology is constantly evolving, our education system must be agile, adaptable, and forward-looking. We must equip our students with the skills they need to navigate the digital future, while also ensuring that our educators have the support they need to lead this transformation."

Singapore's approach demonstrates that leadership is not just about managing change—it's about inspiring and empowering others to embrace it. By providing a clear vision and the resources needed to achieve it, leaders can guide their institutions through the complexities of digital transformation.

The digital revolution in education is not just a technological shift—it's a fundamental change in how we think about learning and teaching. As we've seen, the successful integration of digital technology into education requires a holistic approach that considers the unique challenges and opportunities of each context. Leadership plays a central role in this transformation. Educational leaders must be able to navigate the complexities of digital change, balancing the need for innovation with the imperative to ensure equity and access for all learners. They must also inspire and empower educators to embrace new teaching methodologies and guide students in their journey through the digital landscape.

As we move forward into an increasingly digital future, the role of leadership in education will become even more critical. The decisions made today will shape the future of education for generations to come, and it is incumbent upon leaders to ensure that this future is one where all students have the opportunity to succeed in a digital world.

Key Takeaways

- The digital revolution in education is not just about integrating new tools but fundamentally reshaping how we approach teaching and learning. This shift requires a rethinking of educational practices and the role of educators in guiding students through an increasingly complex digital landscape.

- Digital technology has the power to democratize education, making learning accessible to more people, regardless of location or socio-economic status. Examples like Eneza Education in Africa demonstrate how mobile-based platforms can bridge gaps and provide educational opportunities to underserved communities.
- The digital divide remains a significant barrier to equitable education. Efforts like China's "Internet Plus Education" program highlight the importance of not only providing access to technology but also ensuring that students and educators are equipped to use it effectively.
- As the role of educators shifts from being the sole source of knowledge to facilitators of learning, continuous professional development becomes crucial. Finland's approach to teacher training underscores the importance of equipping educators with the skills needed to thrive in a digital environment.
- Effective leadership is key to navigating the complexities of digital transformation in education. Singapore's success in integrating technology into its education system demonstrates the power of visionary leadership that balances innovation with accountability and fosters a culture of continuous improvement.

CHAPTER II

Understanding Digital Leadership

"The greatest danger in times of turbulence is not the turbulence—it is to act with yesterday's logic. — Peter Drucker"

Consider the modern classroom, where technology is no longer a supplementary tool but a central element of the learning environment. The chalkboards and printed textbooks of the past have given way to tablets, online learning platforms, and virtual classrooms. For educational leaders, this shift isn't just about adopting new tools; it's about rethinking how education itself is delivered. It's about leading with a vision that embraces change and innovation, and about cultivating the skills and mindset necessary to navigate this new landscape. This chapter explores what it takes to be an effective digital leader in this age of transformation, focusing on the skills you need to develop and the mindset shifts that will help you guide your institution through this evolving terrain.

The Transition from Traditional to Digital Leadership

Let's start by acknowledging that traditional leadership models, where decisions were made at the top and filtered down through a rigid hierarchy, don't work as effectively in today's digital world. The speed at which technology is advancing demands a different kind of leadership—one that's flexible, collaborative, and deeply engaged with both the opportunities and challenges that technology brings. Digital leadership is about more than just using technology; it's about creating a vision for how technology can enhance education and then inspiring others to join you on that journey. It's about being open to new ideas, willing to take risks, and ready to adapt when things don't go as planned.

Denmark is a great example of a country that has embraced digital leadership on a national scale. The Danish National Centre for Digital Education (NCDE) has made it a priority to equip educational leaders with the skills and mindset needed to lead in a digital world. What's interesting about Denmark's approach is that it's not just about teaching leaders how to use technology—it's about encouraging them to think creatively about how technology can enhance education. This has led to a culture where innovation is not just encouraged but expected. Lisbeth Knudsen, a leading figure in Danish education, once said, "In a world where technology is constantly changing, the role of the leader is to guide their institution through the unknown, to be both a navigator and an innovator." This mindset is what sets digital leaders apart—they are not just managers; they are visionaries who inspire change.

Essential Skills for Digital Leadership

To be an effective digital leader, there are certain skills that you need to develop. These aren't just technical skills, but a mix of strategic thinking, adaptability, and the ability to manage change.

Being digitally literate doesn't mean you need to be a tech expert, but it does mean you should have a solid understanding of how digital tools work and how they can be used to improve education. It's about knowing enough to make informed decisions and to lead your team with confidence in a digital environment.

At the University of Melbourne, leaders have made digital literacy a cornerstone of their approach to digital transformation. In 2023, they launched a Digital Literacy Initiative designed to give educational leaders the tools they need to navigate the complexities of digital change. Through workshops and online courses, leaders are learning how to use digital tools effectively, not just for administrative tasks, but to truly enhance the learning experience for students. This initiative has empowered leaders to take control of their institution's digital journey, ensuring that technology is used thoughtfully and effectively. It's a reminder that being a digital leader means being comfortable with technology, but more importantly, being curious about its potential.

Strategic Thinking and Vision

Digital leadership also requires strategic thinking. This means not just reacting to changes as they happen, but anticipating them and planning for the future. It's about having a clear vision for where you want your institution to go and developing a roadmap to get there.

South Korea has long been a leader in integrating technology into education. Their "Smart Education" initiative, which began over a decade ago, was one of the first to truly embrace digital learning on a large scale. What's impressive about South Korea's approach is the strategic vision that underpins it. They didn't just implement technology for technology's sake; they had a clear plan for how digital tools would enhance learning and help students develop the skills they need for the future.

This kind of strategic thinking is crucial for digital leaders. It's about seeing the big picture and making decisions today that will benefit your institution tomorrow.

Change Management

Change can be difficult, especially when it involves new technology. As a digital leader, one of your key roles is to manage this change effectively. This means being able to guide your team through the transition, addressing their concerns, and ensuring that everyone is on board with the new direction.

In Japan, where tradition often plays a strong role in education, digital transformation has been a challenge. However, universities like Keio University have managed this change effectively by taking a phased approach. They started with small pilot programs, allowing faculty and students to get used to new technologies gradually before rolling them out more widely. This approach has helped minimize resistance and ensured that the transition to digital learning was smooth and well-received. It's a reminder that change doesn't happen overnight, and that managing it thoughtfully is key to success.

Collaborative Leadership

Gone are the days when leaders made decisions behind closed doors. Today, leadership is about collaboration—working with others, both within your institution and beyond, to drive innovation and achieve shared goals. This means engaging with faculty, students, and even external partners to develop and implement digital strategies.

The Open University in the UK has long been a pioneer in distance education, and their approach to digital transformation is a great example of collaborative leadership. They've established strong partnerships with technology companies, other educational institutions, and government agencies to help develop and implement their digital strategies. What's made the Open University's approach so successful is their commitment to involving all stakeholders in the process. Faculty and students have a say in how digital tools are used, which has helped create a sense of ownership and enthusiasm for the changes taking place.

This kind of collaboration is crucial in digital leadership. By bringing everyone into the conversation, you can ensure that your digital initiatives are not only effective but also embraced by your entire community.

Mindset Shifts for Digital Leadership

Along with developing new skills, becoming a digital leader requires a shift in mindset. This means letting go of old ways of thinking and embracing new approaches that are better suited to today's fast-paced, digital world. One of the biggest mindset shifts for digital leaders is the need to embrace innovation and be willing to take risks. In a world where technology is constantly changing, playing it safe isn't an option. Leaders need to be open to new ideas, willing to experiment with new technologies, and not afraid to fail.

The University of Cape Town (UCT) in South Africa is a great example of an institution that has embraced innovation as part of its digital transformation strategy.

They've created an Innovation Lab where faculty and students can experiment with new technologies and develop creative solutions to educational challenges. This lab has become a hub of creativity, where risk-taking is encouraged, and failure is seen as a learning opportunity. By fostering a culture of innovation, UCT has been able to stay at the forefront of digital education, constantly exploring new ways to enhance learning. This example shows that being a digital leader means being willing to step outside your comfort zone and try new things.

Fostering a Growth Mindset

Another important mindset shift for digital leaders is the adoption of a growth mindset—the belief that skills and abilities can be developed over time, and that challenges are opportunities for growth. Leaders with a growth mindset are more likely to embrace change, take on new challenges, and inspire their teams to do the same.

Nanyang Technological University (NTU) in Singapore has made fostering a growth mindset a key part of its leadership development programs. NTU's leaders are encouraged to view challenges as opportunities to learn and grow, and this approach has been instrumental in helping the university navigate the complexities of digital transformation. By promoting a growth mindset, NTU has created a culture where continuous learning and improvement are valued, which has been critical to the success of their digital initiatives.

Prioritizing Inclusivity and Diversity

Finally, digital leaders must prioritize inclusivity and diversity in their decision-making. This means ensuring that digital initiatives are accessible to all students, regardless of their background or circumstances, and that diverse perspectives are considered in the planning and implementation of digital strategies. The University of British Columbia (UBC) in Canada has made inclusivity and diversity a central focus of its digital transformation efforts. Their Digital Learning Strategy includes specific goals for increasing access to digital resources for underrepresented groups and ensuring that digital tools are designed with inclusivity in mind.

UBC's commitment to diversity and inclusion has helped create a more equitable and inclusive digital learning environment, ensuring that all students can benefit from the university's digital initiatives. This example highlights the importance of considering diversity and inclusion in all aspects of digital leadership.

Being a digital leader in today's world is both challenging and exciting. It requires a unique set of skills and a fundamental shift in mindset, but the rewards are significant. Effective digital leadership is about embracing change, fostering innovation, and working collaboratively to create a vision for the future of education. In a rapidly changing digital landscape, educational leaders must be both visionary strategists and collaborative partners, guiding their institutions through the complexities of digital transformation. By developing the essential skills and adopting the necessary mindset shifts, digital leaders can ensure that their institutions are well-positioned to thrive in the digital age.

Key Takeaways

- Digital leadership isn't just about using new tools—it's about reimagining how education is delivered. Effective leaders embrace a vision for how technology can transform learning and inspire others to join them in that journey.
- Strategic thinking is crucial in navigating the complexities of the digital age. Leaders who anticipate changes and plan for the future, like those in South Korea, ensure their institutions remain competitive and relevant.
- Digital leaders must be willing to innovate and take risks. By fostering a culture of experimentation and learning from failures, leaders can drive continuous improvement and keep their institutions at the cutting edge of education.
- In today's interconnected world, leadership is about collaboration. Engaging with faculty, students, and external partners, as seen at the Open University, is essential for developing and implementing effective digital strategies.
- Prioritizing inclusivity and fostering a growth mindset are critical for successful digital leadership. By ensuring that digital initiatives are accessible to all and viewing challenges as opportunities for growth, leaders can create a more equitable and dynamic educational environment.

CHAPTER III

Strategic Vision and Agile Planning for Digital Transformation

"Strategy is not the consequence of planning, but the opposite: its starting point. — Henry Mintzberg"

Imagine sitting down with your team to plan the future of your institution. You're not just thinking about the next semester or the next year—you're thinking about where your institution needs to be in five, ten, or even twenty years. The challenge isn't just about keeping up with the latest technological trends; it's about crafting a vision that anticipates the future and developing a plan that's flexible enough to adapt to whatever comes your way. That's the essence of strategic vision and agile planning in the context of digital transformation.

In this chapter, we'll explore how to create a forward-thinking strategic vision for your institution's digital transformation, drawing from recent examples around the world. We'll also discuss how to execute that vision with an agile approach, ensuring that your plans can evolve with the changing landscape of education.

The Power of a Strategic Vision

When it comes to digital transformation, a strong strategic vision is your North Star. It's the guiding force that ensures every decision, every project, and every initiative is aligned with your institution's long-term goals. Without it, digital transformation efforts can become disjointed, with different departments pulling in different directions. But with a clear vision, everything falls into place.

Let's take a look at the University of Sydney. In 2023, they launched their "Digital 2025" initiative—a comprehensive plan to integrate digital technologies across the university. But this wasn't just about adopting new tools or platforms; it was about reimagining what education could be in a digital world. Their vision was bold: to enhance the student experience, empower faculty with cutting-edge teaching tools, and streamline administrative processes to create a more efficient and effective institution. Vice-Chancellor Mark Scott captured the essence of their approach when he said, "Our goal is not just to keep pace with technological change, but to lead it." This mindset is crucial. The University of Sydney isn't just reacting to changes—they're shaping their future by aligning their digital initiatives with their broader educational mission.

What we can learn from the University of Sydney is the importance of a vision that goes beyond the immediate future. It's about thinking big, about where you want your institution to be in the long term, and then using that vision to guide your digital transformation efforts.

Crafting a Vision That's Both Bold and Grounded

Creating a strategic vision for digital transformation isn't just about dreaming big—it's about being realistic, too. It involves understanding your institution's strengths and weaknesses, recognizing the opportunities on the horizon, and being honest about the challenges you'll face. This balance between ambition and realism is what makes a vision not only inspiring but also achievable.

IIT Bombay has taken a forward-thinking approach with its "Vision 2030" plan. Launched in 2024, this vision isn't just about integrating digital technologies into their educational processes; it's about leveraging those technologies to address real-world challenges. They've partnered with leading tech companies and research organizations to develop solutions in areas like artificial intelligence, data analytics, and digital learning platforms. Director Subhasis Chaudhuri articulated their vision beautifully: "At IIT Bombay, we see digital transformation as an opportunity to push the boundaries of what's possible in education and research." This approach shows that digital transformation isn't just about keeping up with the latest tech trends; it's about using technology to drive innovation and make a real impact on society.

IIT Bombay's vision is a reminder that a strong strategic vision should be both bold and grounded in reality. It should inspire your institution to reach new heights while also being rooted in a deep understanding of your unique context and capabilities.

The Flexibility of Agile Planning

While having a strategic vision is essential, it's equally important to be flexible in how you achieve it. The educational landscape is constantly changing, and your plans need to be able to adapt to new challenges and opportunities. This is where agile planning comes in. Agile planning is all about flexibility. It's about being responsive to change and being willing to pivot when necessary. Instead of sticking rigidly to a long-term plan, agile planning encourages continuous feedback, iteration, and improvement.

The National University of Singapore (NUS) has embraced agile planning as part of its digital transformation efforts. In 2024, NUS implemented an agile framework that allows them to respond quickly to emerging trends and technological advancements. They use cross-functional teams that bring together expertise from different areas of the university, working in short, iterative cycles to test new ideas and gather feedback. This approach has been incredibly effective for NUS. By remaining flexible and responsive, they've been able to stay at the forefront of digital innovation, continually refining their strategies to meet the evolving needs of their students and faculty.

President Tan Eng Chye of NUS explained the benefits of this approach, saying, "In today's fast-paced world, we need to be able to adapt quickly to new developments. Agile planning allows us to stay ahead of the curve, ensuring that our digital transformation efforts are always aligned with the latest advancements in technology and the changing needs of our community." What NUS teaches us is that agility isn't just a buzzword—it's a crucial strategy for ensuring that your digital transformation efforts remain relevant and effective in a rapidly changing environment.

From Vision to Action

Once you've crafted a strategic vision and embraced agile planning, the next step is to turn that vision into action. Execution is where the rubber meets the road—it's about translating your ideas into tangible outcomes, with clear goals, timelines, and metrics for success.

University College London (UCL) offers a powerful example of how to execute a digital strategy effectively. In 2024, they launched their "Digital UCL" strategy, which aimed to integrate digital technologies across the entire institution. The strategy focused on four key areas: digital education, digital research, digital infrastructure, and digital engagement. To ensure successful execution, UCL established a dedicated Digital Transformation Office (DTO) to oversee all digital initiatives. The DTO works closely with academic departments, administrative units, and external partners to ensure that every project is aligned with the institution's strategic vision. Provost Michael Arthur emphasized the importance of execution in digital transformation, noting, "Having a strategic vision is just the first step. The real challenge is in execution—turning that vision into reality. At UCL, we are committed to ensuring that our digital initiatives are not only ambitious but also achievable, with clear goals and measurable outcomes."

UCL's approach highlights the importance of having a dedicated team and clear processes for execution. It's not enough to have a great vision—you need to have the right people and plans in place to make that vision a reality.

Navigating Challenges Along the Way

Of course, no digital transformation journey is without its challenges. Whether it's resistance to change, budget constraints, or technical difficulties, there will always be obstacles to overcome. The key is to be prepared for these challenges and to have strategies in place to address them.

ETH Zurich, one of Europe's top technical universities, faced significant resistance when it first introduced its digital transformation strategy. Faculty members were concerned that digital technologies would detract from the traditional educational experience, and many were skeptical about the benefits of the new tools being introduced. To overcome this resistance, ETH Zurich took a collaborative approach. They involved faculty in the planning and implementation of digital initiatives, ensuring that their concerns were heard and addressed. The university also invested in extensive training programs to help faculty develop the skills needed to use digital tools effectively in their teaching and research. Rector Sarah Springman reflected on the process, saying, "Digital transformation is not just about technology—it's about people. We recognized early on that for our digital initiatives to succeed, we needed to bring everyone on board. By involving our faculty in the process and providing them with the support they needed, we were able to overcome resistance and create a culture that embraces digital innovation."

ETH Zurich's experience shows that the human element is just as important as the technological one in digital transformation. By engaging stakeholders and providing the necessary support, institutions can overcome resistance and ensure the success of their digital initiatives.

Leadership in Digital Transformation

At the end of the day, digital transformation is about more than just technology—it's about leadership. It's about having the vision to see where your institution needs to go, the flexibility to adapt to changes along the way, and the determination to see your plans through to completion.

Pontificia Universidad Católica de Chile (PUC Chile) has become a leader in digital transformation in Latin America, thanks in large part to the vision and leadership of its rector, Ignacio Sánchez. Under his guidance, PUC Chile has implemented a comprehensive digital transformation strategy that includes the development of new digital learning platforms, the integration of data analytics into decision-making processes, and the expansion of online and hybrid learning opportunities. Rector Sánchez has emphasized the importance of leadership in driving digital transformation, stating, "As leaders, it is our responsibility to guide our institutions through this period of change. This requires not only a clear vision but also the ability to inspire others to embrace that vision and work together to achieve it."

PUC Chile's success highlights the critical role that leadership plays in digital transformation. It's not just about setting the direction—it's about leading by example, fostering collaboration, and supporting continuous innovation.

Strategic vision and agile planning are the cornerstones of successful digital transformation in education. Institutions that embrace these principles are better equipped to navigate the complexities of digital change and achieve long-term success. Crafting a strategic vision that is both ambitious and grounded in reality, adopting an agile approach to planning, and executing your plans with precision and flexibility are all essential steps in this process. And throughout it all, strong leadership is the glue that holds everything together, ensuring that your institution not only adapts to the digital age but thrives in it.

As you move forward in your own digital transformation journey, remember that the path won't always be easy. But with a clear vision, a flexible plan, and a commitment to seeing your goals through, you can guide your institution toward a future where education is more accessible, engaging, and effective than ever before.

Key Takeaways

- A strategic vision is the guiding force behind successful digital transformation. It aligns all efforts, ensuring that every action taken is purposeful and contributes to the long-term goals of the institution. Without a clear vision, digital initiatives can become fragmented and lose direction.

- A strong vision for digital transformation should be both bold and grounded. It's about dreaming big while being realistic about the institution's capabilities and challenges. This balance ensures that the vision is not only inspiring but also achievable.

- In a rapidly changing educational landscape, agile planning is essential. It allows institutions to adapt to new challenges and opportunities, ensuring that digital transformation efforts remain relevant and effective. Agility isn't just about flexibility—it's about staying ahead of the curve.

- Crafting a vision is only the beginning; turning that vision into reality requires strong execution. This means having clear goals, dedicated teams, and measurable outcomes. Successful execution transforms ideas into tangible results, driving the institution toward its strategic objectives.

- Effective digital transformation hinges on strong leadership. It's not just about setting a direction—it's about inspiring others to embrace the vision, fostering collaboration, and ensuring that the institution continues to innovate and evolve. Leadership is the key to navigating the complexities of digital change and guiding the institution to success.

CHAPTER IV

Change Management in Digital Education

"Change is the law of life. And those who look only to the past or present are certain to miss the future.
— John F. Kennedy"

Change is one of the most challenging aspects of leadership, especially in education, where traditions run deep and the familiar often feels safest. But as the digital age sweeps through every corner of society, educational institutions cannot afford to stay stagnant. Digital transformation is not just an option; it's a necessity for institutions that want to remain relevant and prepare their students for the future. However, guiding a university or school through this transformation is no small feat. It requires not only a clear vision and strong leadership but also a deep understanding of the human element—the fears, uncertainties, and resistance that naturally arise in times of change.

In this chapter, we're going to explore what it takes to manage change in the context of digital education. We'll look at how leaders can navigate the complexities of institutional transformation, address resistance with empathy and strategy, and ultimately create a culture that doesn't just accept change, but embraces it. We'll draw on recent examples from around the world to see how different institutions are leading the way, and what lessons we can learn from their experiences.

Understanding the Roots of Resistance

Before we can talk about how to lead change, we need to understand why people resist it in the first place. Resistance to change is a natural human response. It's often rooted in fear—fear of the unknown, fear of losing control, fear of being left behind. In education, these fears can be particularly strong. Teachers and professors who have spent years mastering their craft might worry that new digital tools will undermine their expertise. Students might feel overwhelmed by new technologies, unsure if they'll be able to keep up. Administrators might be concerned about the costs and complexities of implementing new systems.

Let's consider the University of Vienna, which faced significant resistance when it began its digital transformation in 2023. Many faculty members, who had dedicated decades to perfecting their teaching methods, were apprehensive about the shift to digital. They feared that online platforms would dilute the richness of in-person interactions and that they would struggle to adapt to new technologies. Rather than forcing the change, the university leadership took a different approach. They organized a series of open forums where faculty could voice their concerns and discuss potential solutions. These forums weren't just about addressing fears—they were about involving the faculty in the decision-making process. By making educators feel heard and valued, the University of Vienna was able to gradually reduce resistance and build a more collaborative environment for digital transformation.

This approach underscores an important point: resistance is often a sign that people care deeply about their work. When leaders take the time to listen and involve their teams in the process, they can turn resistance into a source of strength rather than a barrier to progress.

Leading Institutional Transformation

Leadership plays a critical role in managing change, especially in the digital realm. A leader's ability to articulate a clear vision for the future, inspire confidence, and provide the necessary resources is what ultimately determines the success of a digital transformation.

Shanghai Jiao Tong University (SJTU) has been at the forefront of digital transformation in China, thanks largely to the leadership of its president, Zhang Jie. Under his guidance, SJTU has rolled out a comprehensive digital strategy that touches every aspect of the university, from online learning platforms to digital research initiatives. What's particularly noteworthy about SJTU's approach is its emphasis on distributed leadership. President Zhang understood early on that for digital transformation to be successful, it needed buy-in not just from the top but from every level of the institution. To foster this, SJTU launched a Digital Leadership Program aimed at training department heads, faculty, and even students to lead digital initiatives within their own spheres.

"Digital transformation is not a top-down process," Zhang often says. "It's a collective effort that requires leadership at every level. Our job as leaders is to empower others to take the initiative and drive change in their own areas." This example from SJTU highlights that effective leadership in digital transformation isn't about issuing directives from above; it's about empowering others to lead and creating an environment where everyone feels responsible for the institution's success.

Building a Culture That Embraces Change

One of the most challenging aspects of change management is shifting the culture of an institution. Educational institutions, with their long-standing traditions and established practices, can be particularly resistant to change. Yet, for digital transformation to succeed, a culture that values innovation, flexibility, and continuous learning is essential.

Lund University in Sweden recognized the need to shift its culture before it could successfully integrate digital tools into its teaching and research. The university's leadership understood that simply introducing new technologies wouldn't be enough—they needed to foster a mindset that welcomed change and saw it as an opportunity rather than a threat. To achieve this, Lund University launched several initiatives aimed at encouraging innovation and experimentation. They set up Innovation Hubs where faculty and students could explore new digital tools and develop creative approaches to teaching. They also introduced an annual Digital Innovation Award to celebrate those who made significant contributions to the university's digital transformation.

Vice-Chancellor Erik Renström explained the university's approach: "We realized that to truly embrace digital transformation, we needed to change the way we think about education. It's not just about using new tools; it's about fostering a culture where innovation and experimentation are part of our DNA." Lund University's experience shows that changing institutional culture is a critical component of successful digital transformation. By making innovation a core value, the university has created an environment where digital change is not only accepted but actively pursued.

Overcoming Resistance Through Communication and Collaboration

Resistance to change often stems from a lack of understanding or fear of the unknown. One of the most effective ways to overcome this resistance is through open communication and collaboration. By involving stakeholders in the planning and implementation process and keeping them informed every step of the way, leaders can build trust and reduce anxiety.

The University of Cape Town (UCT) in South Africa encountered significant resistance when it began its digital transformation strategy in 2022. Faculty members were concerned about the potential impact of digital tools on the quality of education, while students worried about accessibility and the digital divide. To address these concerns, UCT adopted a highly collaborative approach. The university established Digital Transformation Committees that included faculty, students, and administrators, ensuring that all voices were heard in the process. These committees were responsible for gathering feedback, proposing solutions, and communicating progress to the wider university community.

Vice-Chancellor Mamokgethi Phakeng emphasized the importance of collaboration in overcoming resistance: "Change is always challenging, but it becomes much easier when people feel like they're part of the process. By involving our faculty and students in every step of our digital transformation, we've been able to build a stronger, more united institution." UCT's experience illustrates that collaboration and communication are key to overcoming resistance and ensuring the success of digital transformation. By making stakeholders feel involved and valued, leaders can foster a sense of ownership and commitment to the change process.

Providing Support and Resources

Change is difficult, but it's even more so without the right support. When institutions undergo digital transformation, it's crucial to provide the resources and training necessary to help everyone adapt. This includes investing in technology, offering professional development opportunities, and ensuring that there is ongoing support as new systems are implemented.

The University of British Columbia (UBC) in Canada has been a leader in digital transformation, largely due to its commitment to supporting faculty and staff through the transition. When UBC began its digital transformation, it recognized that success depended on more than just adopting new tools—it required a significant investment in training and resources. UBC established the Centre for Digital Learning, where faculty could receive hands-on training with new digital tools and collaborate with instructional designers to create innovative teaching methods. Additionally, UBC created a Digital Transformation Fund that provided grants to departments for investing in new technologies and piloting digital initiatives.

Professor Santa Ono, UBC's former President, highlighted the importance of this support: "Digital transformation is a complex process that requires more than just good intentions. It requires resources, training, and ongoing support to ensure that everyone has the tools they need to succeed." UBC's approach shows that providing the right support and resources is essential for overcoming resistance and ensuring the long-term success of digital transformation initiatives.

Sustaining Momentum and Encouraging Continuous Improvement

Change management doesn't end once the initial transformation is complete. To ensure long-term success, institutions must sustain momentum and foster a culture of continuous improvement. This means regularly evaluating progress, making necessary adjustments, and celebrating successes to keep the institution motivated and engaged.

The University of Auckland in New Zealand took a proactive approach to sustaining its digital transformation efforts. After successfully implementing a range of digital tools and platforms, the university recognized the importance of continuous improvement to keep pace with technological advancements and the evolving needs of its students and faculty. To this end, the University of Auckland established a Continuous Improvement Task Force. This group regularly reviews the university's digital initiatives, gathering feedback from faculty, students, and IT professionals to identify areas for enhancement. The task force's work ensures that the university's digital infrastructure remains cutting-edge and responsive to the community's needs. Vice-Chancellor Dawn Freshwater emphasized the importance of sustaining momentum: "Digital transformation is not a one-time event; it's an ongoing process. By committing to continuous improvement, we ensure that our institution remains agile, innovative, and prepared for the future." The University of Auckland's experience underscores the importance of sustaining momentum and fostering a culture of continuous improvement. By regularly assessing and refining digital initiatives, institutions can ensure they remain relevant and effective in a rapidly changing world.

Managing change is one of the most challenging aspects of digital transformation in education. Successful change management requires a combination of strong leadership, effective communication, and a commitment to providing the necessary support and resources.

Leading institutional transformation and overcoming resistance is not an easy task, but with the right strategies in place, it's possible to create a culture that embraces change and thrives in the digital age. By understanding the roots of resistance, fostering a culture of innovation, involving stakeholders in the process, and sustaining momentum through continuous improvement, educational leaders can guide their institutions through the complexities of digital transformation and position them for long-term success.

Key Takeaways

- Resistance to change often stems from fear and uncertainty. Effective change management requires empathy, active listening, and involving stakeholders in the decision-making process to transform resistance into collaboration.

- Successful digital transformation isn't driven solely from the top. Empowering leaders at every level of the institution fosters a sense of shared responsibility and creates a culture where innovation and change are embraced.
- Building a culture that values innovation and flexibility is essential for digital transformation. Institutions must shift from traditional mindsets to one where experimentation and continuous learning are encouraged and celebrated.
- Open communication and collaboration are vital in overcoming resistance to change. By involving faculty, students, and staff in the process, institutions can build trust, reduce anxiety, and ensure that everyone feels invested in the transformation.
- Digital transformation doesn't end with implementation. Institutions must commit to continuous improvement, regularly evaluating progress and adapting to new challenges to ensure long-term success in the ever-evolving digital landscape.

CHAPTER V

Innovative Teaching Models in the Digital Age

"Tell me and I forget. Teach me and I remember. Involve me and I learn. — Benjamin Franklin"

Think about the last time you learned something new—whether it was a skill, a concept, or even a hobby. Chances are, you didn't just sit in a classroom listening to a lecture. You might have watched a video, read an article online, or even joined a virtual discussion. This blend of different learning experiences is at the heart of how education is evolving in the digital age. Traditional teaching methods are being transformed, making way for more flexible, engaging, and personalized approaches that meet the diverse needs of today's learners.

In this chapter, we'll dive into the innovative teaching models that are reshaping education. We'll explore how blended, hybrid, and emerging pedagogical approaches are not just adding technology to the mix, but fundamentally changing how we think about teaching and learning. These models are helping educators connect with students in ways that were unimaginable just a few years ago, and they're making education more accessible and effective for everyone involved.

The Power of Blended Learning

Blended learning is more than just a buzzword—it's a powerful approach that combines the best of both worlds. By integrating online learning with traditional classroom experiences, blended learning offers flexibility and depth that purely face-to-face or online courses can't match. This model allows students to engage with materials at their own pace online, while still benefiting from the rich, interactive environment of the classroom.

Take Amrita Vishwa Vidyapeetham in India, for example. This university has embraced blended learning through its A-VIEW (Amrita Virtual Interactive eLearning World) platform. Here, students can attend live virtual lectures, participate in discussions, and access resources online, all while enjoying the in-person guidance of their professors. Professor Venkat Rangan, the Vice-Chancellor, has often emphasized the benefits of this approach: "Blended learning allows us to combine the flexibility of online education with the personalized support that only in-person teaching can provide. It's about creating a learning experience that's both dynamic and supportive." What Amrita is doing isn't just about convenience—it's about enhancing the quality of education by providing students with multiple ways to engage with the material. This flexibility is particularly important in a country like India, where access to education can be limited by geographical and socio-economic factors. Blended learning helps bridge that gap, offering students opportunities they might not otherwise have.

The Flexibility of Hybrid Learning

While blended learning mixes online and in-person experiences, hybrid learning takes it a step further by giving students the choice of how they want to learn. In a hybrid model, students can decide whether to attend classes in person or participate online, depending on what works best for them. This model provides unmatched flexibility, making education accessible to a wider range of students, including those balancing work, family, and other commitments.

The Open University in the UK is a perfect example of how hybrid learning can work. For decades, this institution has been a leader in distance education, and its hybrid model continues to set the standard. Students can engage with course materials online, join live virtual classes, and participate in discussions at their own pace. But if they prefer, they can also attend in-person sessions, creating a learning experience that's truly tailored to their needs. Jane Roberts, Director of Learning and Teaching Innovation at The Open University, explains the philosophy behind their approach: "We believe in giving students choices. Whether they're managing a job, a family, or other responsibilities, our hybrid model ensures they can still access a high-quality education on their own terms."

This level of flexibility is especially important in today's world, where students come from diverse backgrounds and face different challenges. By offering multiple ways to learn, The Open University ensures that education is not just a privilege for the few, but an opportunity for all.

Rethinking How We Teach

As technology continues to evolve, so do the ways we teach. Emerging pedagogical approaches are pushing the boundaries of traditional education, creating more engaging, personalized, and effective learning experiences. These new models are not just about using the latest gadgets—they're about reimagining the entire learning process.

One of the most exciting developments in recent years is the flipped classroom model, where the traditional structure of teaching is turned on its head. Instead of using class time for lectures, students at Singapore Management University (SMU) engage with instructional content—such as videos and readings—before coming to class. When they do meet in person, the focus is on discussion, problem-solving, and applying what they've learned. Professor Arnoud De Meyer, who played a key role in implementing this model at SMU, explains, "The flipped classroom maximizes the value of face-to-face interactions. Instead of spending class time on passive learning, we engage students in activities that promote critical thinking and collaboration." The flipped classroom is a powerful example of how teaching can be transformed to better meet the needs of students. By shifting the focus from passive reception to active participation, SMU has created a more dynamic and engaging learning environment.

Another innovative approach gaining traction is gamification, where elements of game design are used to enhance learning. At the University of Helsinki, gamification has been integrated into courses like computer science and mathematics, making challenging subjects more engaging and accessible. By incorporating challenges, leaderboards, and rewards, the university has turned learning into a game—one that students are eager to play. Dr. Teemu Roos, a professor at the university, puts it this way: "Gamification taps into students' natural motivations, making learning more fun and rewarding. It's about turning something that could be daunting into something they look forward to."

The success of gamification at the University of Helsinki shows that learning doesn't have to be serious to be effective. By making education more interactive and enjoyable, universities can help students overcome barriers and achieve their full potential.

At Aalto University in Finland, problem-based learning (PBL) is another approach that's changing the way students learn. In PBL, students work in groups to solve real-world problems, applying knowledge from various disciplines. This method not only helps students understand the material better but also develops critical thinking, collaboration, and problem-solving skills that are essential in today's world. Professor Ilkka Niemelä, President of Aalto University, highlights the importance of this approach: "Problem-based learning prepares students for the challenges they'll face in their careers. It's not just about learning facts—it's about learning how to apply those facts in practical, meaningful ways."

Aalto's commitment to problem-based learning shows how education can move beyond rote memorization and into the realm of real-world application. By focusing on solving problems, students gain skills that will serve them long after they've left the classroom.

The Role of Technology in Transforming Education

Technology is the driving force behind these innovative teaching models. It enables the flexibility, interactivity, and personalization that are hallmarks of modern education. From artificial intelligence to virtual reality, technological advancements are continually opening up new possibilities for how we teach and learn.

At the University of Tokyo, artificial intelligence (AI) is being used to create personalized learning experiences. By analyzing data on students' learning behaviors, the university's AI-driven platforms can tailor educational content to meet individual needs. This ensures that each student gets the support and challenges they need to succeed. Dr. Tatsuya Yamamoto, a leading researcher at the university, explains the impact of AI on education: "AI allows us to move beyond the one-size-fits-all approach. By personalizing learning, we can better support each student's unique journey, helping them overcome challenges and achieve their goals."

The use of AI at the University of Tokyo represents a significant leap forward in the personalization of education. By harnessing technology, the university can offer a more tailored learning experience, ensuring that no student is left behind. The University of Amsterdam is exploring the potential of virtual reality (VR) to enhance the learning experience. In fields such as medicine, architecture, and engineering, VR allows students to immerse themselves in realistic simulations, gaining hands-on experience in a controlled, safe environment. Professor Jan-Bart de Vries, who leads the VR initiative at the university, remarks, "Virtual reality offers a level of immersion that traditional methods can't match. It allows students to practice skills in a safe, realistic environment, which is invaluable in disciplines where hands-on experience is crucial."

The University of Amsterdam's use of VR illustrates how technology can transform education by creating immersive, interactive learning environments. By pushing the boundaries of what's possible, the university is helping students gain the skills and experience they need to excel in their chosen fields.

The Global Impact of Innovative Teaching Models

These innovative teaching models aren't just transforming education in elite institutions—they're having a global impact, making education more accessible, engaging, and effective for learners around the world.

In Kenya, Bridge International Academies is using blended learning to bring high-quality education to underserved communities. By combining digital content with in-person instruction, these academies provide a cost-effective solution that reaches students who might otherwise have limited access to education. Jay Kimmelman, CEO of Bridge International Academies, explains, "Blended learning allows us to deliver a world-class education at a fraction of the cost of traditional schools. It's about making education accessible to everyone, regardless of where they live or their economic circumstances."

Bridge International Academies shows that innovative teaching models have the potential to transform education for all, bridging gaps and creating opportunities for learners in even the most challenging environments.

Oulu University of Applied Sciences has been a leader in hybrid learning, offering flexible education options for working professionals. Their hybrid model allows students to balance their studies with work and family commitments, making education more accessible for adult learners. Rector Jouko Paaso highlights the importance of flexibility in education: "Hybrid learning enables us to reach a broader audience, including those who might not have been able to pursue higher education due to their personal circumstances. It's about making education more inclusive and adaptable to the needs of all students." The experience of Oulu University of Applied Sciences demonstrates the global impact of hybrid learning in making education more flexible and inclusive. By offering different pathways to learning, the university is helping to democratize education and expand opportunities for lifelong learning.

The digital age is transforming education in ways that were once unimaginable. Innovative teaching models like blended, hybrid, and emerging pedagogical approaches are not just changing how we teach—they're redefining what education can be. These models are making learning more accessible, personalized, and engaging, helping students around the world achieve their full potential. These innovative teaching models are having a profound impact on education. They are breaking down barriers, creating new opportunities, and preparing students for the challenges of the modern world.

The future of education lies in our ability to innovate, to embrace new technologies and pedagogical approaches, and to create learning environments that meet the needs of all students. As educational leaders, it is our responsibility to explore these possibilities and to lead our institutions into this exciting new era of teaching and learning.

Key Takeaways

- Blended learning integrates online and in-person education, offering students the flexibility to engage with material at their own pace while still benefiting from the interaction and support of traditional classroom settings. This model enhances the learning experience by providing multiple pathways to understanding and mastery.
- Hybrid learning takes flexibility a step further by allowing students to choose how they want to engage—whether in person or online. This model caters to diverse student needs, making education more accessible to those balancing other commitments, and ensuring that quality learning is available on their terms.
- New pedagogical models like the flipped classroom, gamification, and problem-based learning are transforming how education is delivered. These approaches emphasize active participation, real-world application, and engagement, making learning more relevant and effective for today's students.
- The integration of technologies such as AI and virtual reality is driving the evolution of teaching models, enabling personalized, immersive, and interactive learning experiences. These technologies are not just tools—they are reshaping the very nature of education.
- Innovative teaching models are making education more inclusive and accessible worldwide. Whether it's bringing high-quality education to underserved communities or offering flexible options for working

professionals, these models are democratizing education and expanding opportunities for learners everywhere.

44

CHAPTER VI

Engagement and Motivation in Digital Learning

"The only way to do great work is to love what you do. — Steve Jobs"

Think back to a time when you were completely absorbed in a task, where the hours flew by without you even noticing. Perhaps it was a game, a challenging puzzle, or even a project you were passionate about. This kind of deep engagement is what educators strive to achieve in the classroom. But in the digital age, where distractions are everywhere, keeping students motivated and focused can be a challenge. That's where gamification and interactive tools come into play. These strategies aren't just about making learning fun—they're about tapping into the core of what drives human motivation and making education an experience that students are eager to participate in.

In this chapter, we'll explore how gamification and interactive tools are transforming digital learning. We'll dive into recent examples from around the world, showcasing how these approaches are not just engaging students, but also enhancing their understanding and retention of material. By the end of this chapter, you'll have a deeper appreciation for how these tools can be harnessed to create learning experiences that resonate with students on a personal level.

The Power of Gamification in Education

At its heart, gamification is about taking the elements that make games so captivating—points, levels, challenges, and rewards—and applying them to non-game contexts, like education. When done right, gamification turns learning into an adventure, where students are motivated to push their boundaries, tackle new challenges, and enjoy the journey along the way.

Let's start with an institution that's as historic as it is forward-thinking: Nalanda University in India. In 2024, Nalanda introduced gamified elements into its online courses, particularly in subjects like ancient history and environmental science—areas that students often found daunting. By incorporating quizzes, challenges, and a points system, Nalanda turned these courses into interactive experiences that encouraged students to dig deeper into the material. Dr. Sunaina Singh, Vice-Chancellor of Nalanda University, summed it up beautifully: "Gamification isn't about making learning easier; it's about making it more engaging. We want our students to be curious, to explore, and to feel a sense of accomplishment as they progress." What Nalanda has done is remind us that learning doesn't have to be a passive activity. By making it more interactive and rewarding, they've helped students connect with the material in a way that's both meaningful and enjoyable.

Interactive Tools: Bringing Learning to Life

While gamification adds a layer of motivation, interactive tools provide the hands-on experiences that make learning more tangible. These tools, whether they're virtual simulations, collaborative platforms, or real-time feedback systems, allow students to engage with content in ways that are dynamic and immersive.

Over in Australia, the University of Melbourne has been leading the charge with virtual labs, especially in its science and engineering programs. In 2024, the university expanded its use of these labs, allowing students to conduct experiments and explore scientific concepts in a simulated environment. This means that even if a student can't be in a physical lab, they can still get the practical experience that's so crucial in these fields. Professor Mark Hargreaves, Dean of the Faculty of Science, captured the essence of this approach: "Learning by doing is at the core of scientific education. Virtual labs give our students the freedom to experiment, to make mistakes, and to learn from them—just as they would in a physical lab."

The beauty of these virtual labs is that they make education accessible to all students, regardless of where they are. They break down barriers and allow students to engage deeply with the material, honing their skills in a safe, controlled environment.

Building a Culture of Engagement

Gamification and interactive tools can be incredibly effective, but their success depends on how they're integrated into the broader learning environment. It's not just about adding new features—it's about fostering a culture where students feel supported, motivated, and encouraged to take ownership of their learning.

In South Korea, Seoul National University (SNU) has created an online platform that combines gamified elements with real-time collaboration tools. This platform allows students to work together on projects, share resources, and participate in group challenges, all within a supportive and interactive environment. Professor Kim Soo-hyun, who heads the digital learning initiative at SNU, explained why collaboration is so important: "Learning is a social activity. When students work together, they're not just engaging with the material—they're engaging with each other, building a community that enhances their motivation and understanding."

SNU's platform is a great example of how technology can be used to foster collaboration and build a community of learners. By creating spaces where students can interact and support one another, SNU is helping them stay motivated and engaged throughout their studies.

The Role of Technology in Personalized Learning

Technology isn't just a tool—it's a game-changer in how we approach education. From AI-driven feedback systems to virtual reality experiences, technology allows us to tailor learning to the individual needs of each student, making education more personalized and effective.

In Scotland, the University of Edinburgh has been using AI-powered learning assistants in its online courses. These AI tools provide personalized feedback, suggest additional resources based on student performance, and even offer motivational prompts to keep students on track. Dr. Sheila Riddell, Director of the Centre for Research in Digital Education, highlighted the impact of these AI assistants: "Personalized learning is about meeting students where they are. With AI, we can offer support that's tailored to each student's needs, helping them stay engaged and motivated to succeed."

The use of AI at the University of Edinburgh shows how technology can make learning more responsive and supportive. By providing real-time, personalized feedback, these tools help students overcome challenges and keep moving forward.

Addressing Challenges in Digital Engagement

While gamification and interactive tools offer exciting possibilities, they also come with challenges. Issues like digital access, varying levels of technological literacy, and the risk of over-reliance on gamification can all impact their effectiveness. It's essential for educators to approach these tools thoughtfully, ensuring they enhance rather than detract from the learning experience.

The Open University of Hong Kong (OUHK) recognized early on that for digital tools to be successful, students needed a solid foundation in digital literacy. In 2024, OUHK launched a digital literacy initiative to ensure all students had the skills to fully engage with these tools, regardless of their background. Professor Ricky Kwok, Vice-President of Academic at OUHK, put it simply: "Digital tools are only as effective as the people using them. By investing in digital literacy, we're ensuring that all our students can fully participate in and benefit from the digital learning experience."

OUHK's approach highlights the importance of building digital literacy alongside the adoption of new tools. By leveling the playing field, they're making sure that all students can take full advantage of the opportunities that digital learning offers.

The Global Reach of Gamification and Interactive Tools

The impact of gamification and interactive tools isn't limited to any one region—they're being used around the world to make education more engaging, accessible, and effective. From urban universities to rural schools, these tools are helping students connect with their education in new and meaningful ways.

In Colombia, Universidad de los Andes has been using gamified learning modules to enhance education in rural areas. These modules, designed to be accessible on low-cost devices, make subjects like mathematics and science more engaging for students who might otherwise struggle to stay interested. Dr. Pablo Navas, Rector of Universidad de los Andes, reflected on the impact: "Education should be engaging, no matter where you are. By making learning interactive and rewarding, we're helping students in even the most remote areas connect with their education and see its value." Universidad de los Andes shows us that gamification isn't just a tool for making learning fun—it's a way to make education more inclusive and equitable. By reaching students in underserved areas, these tools are helping to close the educational gap and give all students the opportunity to succeed.

Engagement and motivation are at the heart of effective learning, especially in the digital age. Gamification and interactive tools offer powerful ways to enhance these aspects of education, turning learning into an experience that's not just educational but also enjoyable and fulfilling. From Nalanda University's gamified courses to the University of Melbourne's virtual labs, these strategies are making learning more dynamic and accessible for students everywhere. These tools are transforming education on a global scale. They're not just changing how we teach—they're changing how students learn, making education more personalized, inclusive, and engaging.

However, it's important to remember that these tools are just one part of the equation. Successful digital engagement requires thoughtful integration, support for digital literacy, and a commitment to creating learning environments that truly resonate with students. By approaching gamification and interactive tools with intention and care, educators can harness their full potential to create a brighter, more engaging future for education.

Key Takeaways

- By integrating game-like elements into education, gamification turns learning into an engaging journey where students are motivated to take on challenges and enjoy the process of discovery. This approach not only makes learning more enjoyable but also fosters a deeper connection with the material.
- Tools like virtual labs and collaborative platforms make education more tangible and accessible. They allow students to engage with content in dynamic ways, offering hands-on experiences that deepen understanding and make learning more meaningful.
- The effectiveness of gamification and interactive tools depends on their integration into a broader culture of engagement. When students feel supported, motivated, and connected to their peers, their learning experience

is enriched, leading to better outcomes.

- Advances in technology, such as AI-powered feedback systems, enable personalized learning experiences that cater to the unique needs of each student. These tools make education more responsive, helping students stay motivated and on track.
- While digital tools offer exciting possibilities, their success hinges on addressing challenges like digital literacy and access. By ensuring that all students have the skills and resources needed to engage with these tools, educators can create a more inclusive and equitable learning environment.

CHAPTER VII

Building the Digital Foundation

*"Technology is best when it brings people together.
— Matt Mullenweg"*

Imagine a university bustling with students, professors, and staff, all seamlessly connected through a web of digital tools and platforms. Classrooms are equipped with interactive screens, lectures are streamed to students across the globe, and every aspect of the campus, from admissions to alumni relations, is powered by a robust digital infrastructure. This is not just the vision of a futuristic campus; it's the reality for many educational institutions today. But getting there doesn't happen overnight—it requires careful planning, investment, and a commitment to building a digital foundation that supports every aspect of the educational experience.

In this chapter, we're going to explore how institutions around the world are laying the groundwork for this digital transformation. We'll look at the nuts and bolts of what it takes to build and maintain the infrastructure that makes modern education possible. From the challenges of integrating new technologies to the critical importance of cybersecurity, this chapter will offer insights into the real-world efforts of universities and colleges striving to keep up with the digital age.

The Bedrock of a Digital Campus

At the heart of every digital campus is a strong, reliable infrastructure. This isn't just about having fast Wi-Fi or up-to-date computers—though those are certainly important. It's about creating an interconnected system that allows all parts of the institution to function smoothly, from online learning platforms to research databases to administrative software. Without this foundation, even the most innovative educational tools can falter.

Let's start with the University of Tokyo, a leader in educational innovation in Asia. In 2024, the university completed a comprehensive upgrade of its digital infrastructure, recognizing that its existing systems couldn't keep pace with the demands of modern education. The overhaul included the installation of high-speed, reliable internet across all its campuses, the deployment of cloud-based collaboration platforms, and the implementation of advanced cybersecurity measures to protect sensitive information. Dr. Makoto Gonokami, President of the University of Tokyo, spoke about the significance of these upgrades: "A strong digital infrastructure isn't just a nice-to-have—it's essential. It's what enables us to provide our students and faculty with the tools they need to excel in a rapidly changing world." This example underscores a critical point: without a solid digital foundation, universities cannot hope to compete on a global scale. The University of Tokyo's investment in its infrastructure is a clear indication of its commitment to maintaining its position as a leader in education and research.

Weaving Technology into the Fabric of Education

Infrastructure is the foundation, but the real magic happens when technology is woven into the very fabric of teaching and learning. It's not just about adding digital tools to the classroom; it's about creating a seamless integration where technology enhances the educational experience, making it more engaging, personalized, and effective.

In Finland, the University of Turku is pioneering the use of digital learning environments that blend technology into every aspect of education. In 2024, the university launched its "Future Classroom" initiative, which combines interactive whiteboards, virtual reality, and AI-driven learning analytics to create a truly immersive learning experience. Professor Jukka Korpela, who leads this initiative, shared the philosophy behind it: "Our students are digital natives—they expect technology to be an integral part of their education. By integrating these tools into our teaching, we're not just keeping up with the times; we're preparing our students for the future." What the University of Turku is doing goes beyond simply using technology—it's about creating a learning environment where digital tools are a natural extension of the educational process. This kind of integration not only makes learning more dynamic but also ensures that students are equipped with the skills they'll need in a digital workforce.

Overcoming the Hurdles of Digital Transformation

Of course, building this kind of infrastructure isn't without its challenges. Budget constraints, resistance to change, and the complexity of modernizing legacy systems can all stand in the way. But as difficult as these challenges are, they're not insurmountable. With the right approach, institutions can overcome these obstacles and successfully transform their digital capabilities.

Take the University of Cape Town (UCT) in South Africa, for example. In 2024, UCT embarked on a major project to upgrade its digital infrastructure, which had been struggling to keep up with the demands of a growing student population and the need for more advanced digital tools. The project faced numerous challenges, including securing funding, managing the logistics of upgrading infrastructure across multiple campuses, and addressing the concerns of faculty and staff who were wary of the changes. Dr. Mamokgethi Phakeng, Vice-Chancellor of UCT, reflected on the process: "Upgrading our infrastructure was a daunting task, but we knew it was necessary. We had to be creative in finding solutions, from forming partnerships with tech companies to applying for government grants. But most importantly, we made sure to bring everyone on board, ensuring that our faculty and staff felt supported throughout the transition."

UCT's experience highlights the importance of clear communication, careful planning, and creative problem-solving in overcoming the hurdles of digital transformation. The university's successful upgrade has already begun to pay off, enabling it to offer enhanced learning opportunities and positioning it as a leading institution in

Africa.

Securing the Digital Campus: The Role of Cybersecurity

As educational institutions become more digitally integrated, the importance of cybersecurity cannot be overstated. Protecting sensitive data, whether it's student records, research data, or intellectual property, is critical in today's digital landscape. A strong cybersecurity strategy is not just about preventing breaches—it's about building trust and ensuring that students and staff can use digital tools with confidence.

ETH Zurich, one of Europe's leading technical universities, has taken cybersecurity to the next level. In 2024, the university launched a comprehensive cybersecurity initiative that included the deployment of AI-driven threat detection systems, extensive training for staff and students, and the establishment of a dedicated cybersecurity operations center. Dr. Sarah Springman, Rector of ETH Zurich, emphasized why this initiative is so important: "In today's world, cybersecurity isn't just a technical issue—it's a fundamental part of our digital infrastructure. We're committed to staying ahead of the curve, ensuring that our systems are not only secure but resilient against the ever-evolving landscape of cyber threats."

ETH Zurich's approach to cybersecurity demonstrates that protecting a digital campus requires ongoing vigilance and investment. By prioritizing cybersecurity, the university is safeguarding its reputation and ensuring that its digital infrastructure remains a reliable resource for students and staff.

Sustainability and Scalability

As technology continues to advance, educational institutions need to ensure that their digital infrastructure can keep up. This means building systems that are both sustainable and scalable—capable of growing and evolving with the institution's needs without requiring constant overhauls. It also means considering the environmental impact of digital infrastructure, finding ways to reduce energy consumption and carbon footprints.

The National University of Singapore (NUS) is leading the charge in creating sustainable digital infrastructure. In 2024, NUS implemented a campus-wide "Green IT" initiative aimed at reducing the environmental impact of its digital systems. This included the use of energy-efficient servers, adopting cloud-based solutions to minimize the need for physical data centers, and integrating renewable energy sources to power its infrastructure. Professor Tan Eng Chye, President of NUS, spoke about the significance of this initiative: "As a global leader in education, we have a responsibility to lead by example. Our Green IT initiative is about more than just reducing our carbon footprint—it's about building a digital infrastructure that is sustainable, scalable, and ready for the future."

NUS's commitment to sustainability in its digital infrastructure is a powerful reminder that educational institutions must consider not just the present but also the future. By investing in green technologies and scalable systems, universities can build infrastructure that supports their growth while minimizing their environmental impact.

The Future of Digital Infrastructure in Education

The digital landscape is constantly evolving, and so too must the infrastructure that supports it. As we look to the future, educational institutions will need to remain agile, continuously updating their systems to incorporate emerging technologies like AI, quantum computing, and the Internet of Things (IoT). Those institutions that are willing to invest in the future and embrace innovation will be best positioned to lead in the digital age.

The Massachusetts Institute of Technology (MIT) is already preparing for the next wave of digital infrastructure. In 2024, MIT announced an ambitious initiative to explore the integration of quantum computing into its digital systems. While still in its early stages, this project has the potential to revolutionize research and education, offering unprecedented computing power and the ability to solve complex problems that are currently beyond our reach. Dr. Rafael Reif, President of MIT, explained the potential impact of this technology: "Quantum computing represents a paradigm shift in how we think about computation. By investing in this technology now, we're not just preparing for the future—we're helping to shape it." MIT's forward-thinking approach highlights the importance of continuous innovation in digital infrastructure. As new technologies emerge, institutions that are willing to adapt and invest in the future will be best equipped to lead in a rapidly changing world.

Building a robust digital foundation is no longer a luxury—it's a necessity for educational institutions in the modern world. From the University of Tokyo's cutting-edge systems to the National University of Singapore's sustainable initiatives, institutions around the globe are demonstrating what it takes to establish and maintain a strong digital infrastructure. By focusing on integration, cybersecurity, sustainability, and future-readiness, these institutions are not only enhancing their educational offerings but also preparing themselves to meet the demands of tomorrow.

As we move forward, the challenge for educators and administrators is to stay ahead of the curve, ensuring that their systems are not only up-to-date but also capable of supporting the next generation of learners. By building a strong digital foundation today, institutions can ensure their success in the digital age, providing students with the tools and opportunities they need to thrive.

Key Takeaways

- A robust digital infrastructure is the backbone of any educational institution in the digital age. It ensures that all aspects of the institution—from online learning platforms to research and administration—function smoothly, enabling institutions to compete on a global scale.
- Successfully integrating technology into teaching and learning goes beyond simply adding digital tools; it involves creating an environment where technology seamlessly enhances the educational experience, making learning more engaging, personalized, and effective.
- Building a digital infrastructure comes with challenges such as budget constraints and resistance to change.

However, with careful planning, clear communication, and creative problem-solving, institutions can successfully navigate these hurdles and achieve digital transformation.

- As institutions become more digitally integrated, robust cybersecurity measures are essential to protect sensitive data and ensure that digital tools remain reliable and secure. Investing in cybersecurity is crucial for building trust and maintaining a resilient digital infrastructure.

- Educational institutions must design their digital infrastructure to be sustainable and scalable, ensuring it can grow and evolve with future demands while minimizing environmental impact. Investing in green technologies and future-proof systems is vital for long-term success.

Digital Equity and Inclusion

"Technology is a great equalizer only when it is equally accessible. — Sundar Pichai"

In today's digitally-driven world, the potential for technology to revolutionize education is immense. From personalized learning experiences to global collaborations, the possibilities seem endless. However, as we embrace these opportunities, it's essential to confront a significant challenge: not everyone has equal access to these digital resources. This disparity—commonly referred to as the "digital divide"—isn't just about having or not having devices; it's about whether every student, regardless of their background, can access and benefit from digital education. Ensuring digital equity and inclusion has become one of the most urgent tasks for educators and policymakers alike.

This chapter delves into the heart of digital equity, exploring the barriers that prevent students from fully participating in the digital age and examining how different regions around the world are tackling these challenges. We'll look at the successes, the ongoing struggles, and the lessons learned from various initiatives aimed at closing the digital divide. The goal is to understand how we can create a more inclusive digital educational landscape, one where every student has the tools they need to succeed.

Understanding Digital Equity and Inclusion

Digital equity is about more than just providing a laptop or an internet connection; it's about ensuring that every student has the opportunity to fully engage in the digital learning experience. This means considering factors like access to high-quality digital content, the ability to navigate and use technology effectively, and the support systems in place to help students and teachers adapt to new tools.

The COVID-19 pandemic brought this issue into sharp focus. When schools around the world were forced to switch to online learning, the disparities in access to technology became glaringly apparent. In many cases, students who lacked reliable internet connections or digital devices were left behind, struggling to keep up with their peers who had better access. The pandemic was a wake-up call, highlighting the critical need for digital equity in education. Take, for example, India's Pradhan Mantri Gramin Digital Saksharta Abhiyan (PMGDISHA). This ambitious initiative was launched with the goal of making six crore rural households digitally literate. In a country as vast and diverse as India, where the digital divide is stark, PMGDISHA represents a significant effort to bring digital literacy to some of the most underserved communities. What's particularly notable about PMGDISHA is its community-based approach. Training centers have been set up in villages, often run in partnership with local NGOs and educational institutions. These centers offer basic digital literacy courses, teaching participants how to use the internet, send emails, and access government services online. For many in these rural areas, this is their first experience with digital technology.

However, the success of PMGDISHA has not come without challenges. Reaching the most remote areas, where infrastructure is lacking, has been a significant hurdle. Moreover, ensuring that digital literacy translates into meaningful use—such as accessing educational content or improving livelihoods—remains an ongoing task. Yet, the program's impact is undeniable, providing a foundation for digital inclusion in regions where it was previously unimaginable.

The Challenges of Achieving Digital Equity

Despite the strides made by initiatives like PMGDISHA, achieving digital equity is no easy feat. The digital divide is not just a problem of access; it encompasses a range of issues, from socio-economic disparities to varying levels of digital literacy and the availability of supportive infrastructure. In many parts of the world, simply getting online is a challenge. According to data from the World Bank, nearly half of the world's population still lacks access to the internet. This issue is particularly pronounced in rural and low-income areas, where infrastructure is either non-existent or prohibitively expensive to install. Without a reliable internet connection, students in these areas are at a severe disadvantage when it comes to participating in digital learning.

Consider the situation in the United States, where the "homework gap" has become a growing concern. The term refers to the difficulties that students face when they don't have reliable internet access or digital devices at home to complete their homework. This gap is especially wide in low-income and rural communities, where students often have to go to great lengths—such as sitting outside public libraries or fast-food restaurants with free Wi-Fi—to get their work done. The COVID-19 pandemic brought this issue into stark relief. When schools transitioned to remote learning, the homework gap quickly became a crisis. School districts scrambled to provide laptops and Wi-Fi hotspots to students in need, but these stopgap measures highlighted deeper, systemic inequities. While some students were able to continue their education seamlessly from home, others were left struggling to catch up, their learning disrupted by a lack of resources.

The situation in the United States serves as a reminder that digital equity is not just a challenge for developing countries; it's an issue that affects even the most technologically advanced nations. Ensuring that all students have access to the tools they need to learn requires a concerted effort from educators, policymakers, and communities.

The Digital Divide

In Southeast Asia, the digital divide presents a complex challenge. The region is economically diverse, with countries like Singapore and Malaysia boasting well-developed digital infrastructures, while others like Myanmar and Laos lag far behind. In these less developed nations, limited internet penetration and the high cost of digital devices pose significant barriers to digital education. To address these disparities, the ASEAN Digital Masterplan 2025 has been launched, aiming to increase internet access, improve digital literacy, and support the development of digital infrastructure across the region. The masterplan represents a collaborative effort among Southeast Asian nations to bridge the digital divide, recognizing that regional cooperation is essential for creating a more equitable digital landscape.

However, the road to digital equity in Southeast Asia is fraught with challenges. While urban areas in countries like Vietnam and Thailand are rapidly catching up with global digital trends, rural areas remain largely disconnected. Bridging this gap will require not only infrastructure development but also targeted policies that address the specific needs of these underserved communities.

Strategies for Promoting Digital Equity and Inclusion

Addressing the digital divide requires a multi-pronged approach that tackles both the immediate barriers to access and the broader systemic issues that contribute to inequality. This means investing in infrastructure, providing digital literacy training, and fostering partnerships between governments, educational institutions, and the private sector.

One example of a large-scale effort to promote digital equity is Australia's National Broadband Network (NBN). The NBN is a government initiative designed to provide high-speed internet access to all Australians, regardless of where they live. The goal is to ensure that even those in remote and rural areas have the same opportunities to access digital resources as their urban counterparts. The NBN has not been without its challenges. Delays in implementation and debates over the choice of technology have plagued the project. However, the NBN represents a significant step forward in addressing the digital divide in Australia. By prioritizing infrastructure development, the Australian government has laid the foundation for a more inclusive digital education system.

What makes the NBN particularly impactful is its focus on reaching underserved communities. In remote areas where internet access was once a luxury, students are now able to participate in online learning, access educational resources, and connect with peers and teachers from across the country. This has opened up new possibilities for education in regions where opportunities were previously limited.

In Kenya, the Digital Literacy Program (DLP) is another example of an initiative aimed at bridging the digital divide. Launched as part of Kenya's Vision 2030 development agenda, the DLP seeks to equip primary school students with digital devices and provide them with the skills they need to thrive in a digital world. A key component of the DLP is its focus on teacher training. Recognizing that technology is only as effective as the people who use it, the program invests in building the capacity of educators to integrate digital tools into their teaching. This has not only improved digital literacy among students but has also empowered teachers to take full advantage of the opportunities offered by digital education.

Kenya's approach demonstrates the importance of viewing digital equity as more than just access to technology. It's about creating an environment where both students and educators are equipped to use these tools effectively. By focusing on training and support, the DLP is helping to create a generation of digitally literate citizens who can fully participate in the digital economy.

The Role of Policy and Leadership in Promoting Digital Equity

Educational leaders and policymakers have a crucial role to play in driving digital equity. Their decisions shape the policies, investments, and initiatives that determine whether all students have the opportunity to benefit from digital education.

Finland, known for its high-performing education system, has made digital inclusion a central part of its educational strategy. The Finnish government has implemented policies to ensure that all students have access to digital devices and high-quality digital content. From an early age, digital literacy is integrated into the curriculum, ensuring that students develop the skills they need to navigate a digital world. What sets Finland apart is its holistic approach to digital inclusion. The government works closely with schools, municipalities, and private sector partners to create a supportive ecosystem for digital education. This collaboration ensures that digital equity is not just a policy goal but a reality for all Finnish students.

Finland's success highlights the importance of coordinated, systemic efforts to promote digital equity. By involving all stakeholders and addressing the issue from multiple angles, Finland has created an educational environment where digital tools are accessible and beneficial to everyone.

At a broader level, the European Union (EU) has also taken significant steps to promote digital equity through its Digital Education Action Plan. The plan outlines a comprehensive strategy to support digital education across member states, focusing on improving digital skills, enhancing digital infrastructure, and promoting inclusive education. A key element of the action plan is the Digital Skills and Jobs Coalition, which brings together stakeholders from governments, industry, education, and civil society to address the digital skills gap in Europe. The coalition works to ensure that all Europeans, regardless of age or background, have the skills needed to thrive in the digital economy.

The EU's approach underscores the importance of collaboration in promoting digital equity. By bringing together diverse stakeholders, the EU is working to create a more inclusive digital education system that benefits all citizens.

Digital equity and inclusion are essential for ensuring that all students have the opportunity to succeed in a rapidly changing world. As technology becomes increasingly central to education, addressing the digital divide has never been more critical. Through a combination of policy, infrastructure development, community engagement, and partnerships, educational leaders can work toward a future where digital tools and resources are accessible to everyone. While the challenges are significant, they are not insurmountable. With the right strategies and a commitment to equity, educational institutions can ensure that all students have the opportunity to participate fully in the digital age.

As we look to the future, the focus must remain on creating inclusive educational systems that recognize and address the diverse needs of all students. By doing so, we can harness the power of technology to bridge gaps, expand opportunities, and create a more equitable future for education.

Key Takeaways

- Digital equity isn't just about providing devices or internet access; it's about ensuring that every student can fully engage with and benefit from digital education, regardless of their background or location.
- The digital divide is a complex issue that affects both developed and developing countries. Socio-economic disparities, rural access, and digital literacy gaps all contribute to unequal opportunities in education.
- Countries around the world, from India to Finland, are implementing innovative strategies to bridge the digital divide. These efforts highlight the importance of tailored approaches that consider local contexts and needs.
- Effective leadership and thoughtful policy-making are crucial in driving digital equity. Collaborative efforts between governments, educational institutions, and private sectors can create inclusive environments where all students have the tools to succeed.
- Achieving digital equity requires a commitment to continuous improvement, focusing on infrastructure, training, and inclusive policies. By addressing the diverse needs of students, we can build a future where technology empowers every learner, closing gaps and expanding opportunities for all.

CHAPTER IX

Data-Driven Decision Making

"Without data, you're just another person with an opinion. — W. Edwards Deming"

Imagine a classroom where every decision, from how lessons are structured to how resources are allocated, is informed by data. It's not just a dream—it's the reality that many educational institutions are striving toward today. In an era where technology touches almost every aspect of our lives, the ability to collect, analyze, and act on data has become a powerful tool in shaping the future of education. But with this power comes a responsibility to use data wisely, ensuring that it serves to enhance learning and support students, rather than reduce them to mere numbers on a spreadsheet.

This chapter delves into the world of data-driven decision-making in education. It explores how schools and universities can harness data to make informed decisions that improve student outcomes, optimize resources, and support teachers in their vital work. Along the way, we'll look at some of the challenges involved in adopting a data-driven approach, including the ethical considerations that must be carefully navigated. Through examples from around the world, we'll see how different institutions are successfully using data to drive meaningful change, while also understanding the complexities that come with it.

The Power of Data in Education

Data has always been a part of education—think about test scores, attendance records, and graduation rates. But today, the landscape has changed dramatically. With digital tools and platforms, educators now have access to a wealth of data that can offer insights far beyond traditional metrics. This data can reveal patterns in student behavior, highlight areas where learners are struggling, and even predict future outcomes. For educational leaders, this information is invaluable, providing a solid foundation upon which to build strategies that are not just reactive but proactive. In Australia, the National Assessment Program – Literacy and Numeracy (NAPLAN) has been a significant source of data for educators. Each year, students in Years 3, 5, 7, and 9 are tested on their literacy and numeracy skills, and the data collected is used to assess the overall health of the education system. Schools can see how their students are performing compared to national benchmarks, and they can identify areas where improvements are needed. But it's not just about the numbers—NAPLAN data has sparked important conversations about how to best support students who are falling behind, leading to targeted interventions that address specific needs.

However, the use of data isn't without its challenges. While NAPLAN has provided valuable insights, it has also faced criticism. Some argue that the pressure to perform on these standardized tests can be detrimental to students' well-being, and there is concern that an over-reliance on data can reduce education to a series of metrics. This highlights the importance of using data thoughtfully, ensuring that it enhances education rather than detracts from the holistic experience of learning.

The Challenges of Implementing Data-Driven Decision Making

Embracing a data-driven approach in education sounds great in theory, but in practice, it comes with its own set of challenges. Collecting data is one thing; turning it into actionable insights is another. Many schools struggle with integrating different data systems—attendance, grades, behavior tracking, and more—into a cohesive whole. Without this integration, the full potential of data remains untapped.

Take the Los Angeles Unified School District (LAUSD) in the United States, for example. LAUSD is one of the largest school districts in the country, serving hundreds of thousands of students. To better understand their needs, the district invested in a comprehensive data integration platform. This system pulls together information from various sources, allowing educators to see real-time data on student performance, attendance, and even social-emotional well-being. The idea is to provide a complete picture of each student, helping teachers and administrators make more informed decisions. But the road to this kind of integration wasn't easy. LAUSD faced numerous hurdles, from technical issues to resistance from staff who were unfamiliar with the new tools. It became clear that successful data integration isn't just about having the right technology—it's about ensuring that everyone involved is on board and knows how to use the tools effectively. This required extensive training and ongoing support, but the results have been promising, with more personalized interventions and improved student outcomes.

There's also the issue of data overload. With so much information available, it can be overwhelming for educators to know where to start. The key is not just to collect data, but to filter and analyze it in a way that is meaningful and actionable. This is where data literacy becomes crucial—teachers and administrators need to be equipped with the skills to interpret data correctly and apply it in their daily decision-making.

Ethical Considerations in Data Usage

With the increasing reliance on data, ethical considerations have come to the forefront. How do we ensure that data is used responsibly, especially when it comes to sensitive information about students? The potential for misuse is a real concern—data could be used to unfairly label students, reinforce biases, or invade privacy. Educational leaders must tread carefully, balancing the benefits of data-driven decision-making with the rights and well-being of students. In the United Kingdom, learning analytics has become a widely adopted tool in higher education. Universities collect data on student behavior—such as how often they log into online platforms, their participation in class, and their grades—to identify those who might be at risk of dropping out. The idea is to provide early interventions that can help students stay on track. For instance, the University of Edinburgh has implemented a system that tracks student engagement and uses this data to offer tailored support to those who may be struggling.

While this approach has had positive outcomes, it has also sparked debate. Critics argue that tracking students so closely can feel intrusive and that it might lead to a "big brother" scenario where students feel constantly monitored. To address these concerns, the University of Edinburgh has established a clear data governance framework. This framework outlines how data will be used, who has access to it, and how students can opt out if they wish. By being transparent and putting safeguards in place, the university is working to balance the benefits of learning analytics with the need to respect students' privacy. This example illustrates that ethical considerations must be an integral part of any data-driven strategy. It's not just about what data can do, but about how it's used—and ensuring that it serves the best interests of all students.

Data-Driven Decision Making in Action

Despite the challenges, many educational institutions around the world are successfully using data to drive positive change. These success stories provide valuable insights into what works and how others might follow suit.

Singapore is often held up as a model for educational excellence, and its use of data is a big part of that success. The Singapore Ministry of Education collects a wide range of data, from academic performance to student feedback, and uses it to inform everything from curriculum development to teacher training. What sets Singapore apart is its holistic approach—data is not just used to assess students, but to support them. For example, schools in Singapore use data to identify students who might need extra help, whether it's with academic subjects or emotional support. Rather than stigmatizing these students, the focus is on providing targeted interventions that help them succeed. This could mean additional tutoring, counseling services, or adjustments to the curriculum to better meet their needs. The result is a system where data is seen as a tool for growth, not judgment, and where every student has the opportunity to thrive.

Another success story comes from India, where the DIKSHA platform is making waves in the education sector. DIKSHA, which stands for Digital Infrastructure for Knowledge Sharing, is a national platform that provides teachers with access to digital resources and tools. But it's more than just a repository of information—DIKSHA collects data on how these resources are used, offering insights into what works and what doesn't. One of the key features of DIKSHA is its ability to provide real-time feedback to teachers. This means that educators can see how their students are engaging with the material and make adjustments on the fly. If a particular lesson isn't resonating, the teacher can quickly pivot and try a different approach. This data-driven flexibility has led to improvements in teaching quality and student outcomes across India. Moreover, the data collected through DIKSHA is used by policymakers to identify gaps in the education system and allocate resources more effectively.

These examples from Singapore and India highlight the potential of data-driven decision-making to create more responsive and personalized educational environments. By using data to inform their decisions, educators can better meet the needs of their students, leading to improved outcomes and a more equitable education system.

Looking to the Future

As technology continues to advance, the possibilities for data-driven decision-making in education are expanding. Emerging technologies like artificial intelligence (AI) and machine learning offer new ways to analyze data and gain insights that were previously unimaginable. These tools can help educators personalize learning experiences, predict student outcomes, and even automate administrative tasks, freeing up time for teachers to focus on what they do best—teaching. China has been a leader in integrating AI into its education system. Companies like TAL Education Group and Squirrel AI are using AI to create personalized learning experiences that adapt to each student's needs. By analyzing data on how students interact with the material—what they find challenging, how they progress, and where they excel—these systems can tailor lessons to ensure that every student is learning at their own pace.

The potential of AI in education is vast, but it also raises new challenges and ethical questions. For example, how do we ensure that AI systems are fair and unbiased? How do we protect the privacy of students whose data is being used to train these systems? And how do we ensure that the benefits of AI are accessible to all, not just those in well-resourced schools?

As educational leaders explore the possibilities of AI and other emerging technologies, it's crucial that they approach these tools with a critical eye. The goal should always be to enhance education, not replace the human elements that make learning so powerful.

Data-driven decision-making has the potential to transform education, offering educators the insights they need to improve student outcomes and create more effective learning environments. But as with any powerful tool, it must be used thoughtfully and ethically. Educational leaders must navigate the challenges of data integration, ensure that data is used responsibly, and keep the focus on supporting students, not just measuring them. While the journey to data-driven decision-making is complex, it's also filled with opportunities. By embracing data and using it to inform their decisions, educators can create more responsive, adaptive, and equitable educational systems that prepare students for success in the digital age.

As we move forward, the role of data in education will only continue to grow. The challenge for educators and policymakers will be to harness this power in a way that truly benefits all students, ensuring that data-driven decision-making leads to more than just better metrics—it leads to better learning.

Key Takeaways

- Data-driven decision-making has the potential to revolutionize education by providing insights that can improve student outcomes, optimize resources, and personalize learning experiences. However, it must be used thoughtfully to enhance education rather than reduce it to mere numbers.
- Integrating data systems and ensuring that educators are equipped to use data effectively are significant challenges. Successful data-driven decision-making requires not just the right technology, but also ongoing training, support, and a commitment to overcoming resistance to change.
- The use of data in education comes with ethical responsibilities. It's essential to protect student privacy, ensure data is used fairly, and avoid reinforcing biases. Transparency and clear governance are key to navigating these ethical challenges.

- Examples from around the world, such as Singapore's holistic approach and India's DIKSHA platform, demonstrate that data-driven strategies can lead to meaningful improvements in education. These stories show the importance of using data to support students rather than judge them.
- Emerging technologies like AI offer exciting possibilities for data-driven education but also bring new challenges. As these technologies evolve, educators must ensure they are used in ways that enhance learning and benefit all students, not just a select few.

CHAPTER X

Professional Development for Digital Competence

"Leadership and learning are indispensable to each other. — John F. Kennedy"

Imagine walking into a classroom where the professor is not just an expert in their field but also seamlessly integrates digital tools to enhance the learning experience. They might use interactive simulations to explain complex concepts, incorporate real-time feedback tools to gauge student understanding, and create a dynamic online environment that keeps students engaged even outside the classroom. This isn't just a glimpse into the future—it's happening now in institutions that have embraced the need for professional development in digital competence.

As we navigate the digital age, the role of educators in higher education is evolving rapidly. It's no longer enough to just deliver lectures or manage a course syllabus. Today's educators are expected to be digitally savvy, able to use technology not just as a supplement to their teaching but as a core component of it. But how do we get there? How do we ensure that educators are equipped to meet these new demands? This chapter explores how institutions around the world are tackling these challenges, the impact it's having, and why this journey is so crucial for the future of higher education.

The Need for Digital Competence in Today's Education Landscape

We live in a world where technology is omnipresent, and higher education is no exception. Students today are digital natives—they've grown up with the internet, smartphones, and social media. They expect their learning experiences to be just as interactive, responsive, and connected as the rest of their lives. For educators, this means that mastering digital tools isn't just a nice-to-have; it's essential. Digital competence goes beyond knowing how to use a computer or navigate a learning management system. It's about understanding how to leverage technology to create richer, more engaging learning experiences. It's about using data to inform teaching practices, creating digital content that resonates with students, and even understanding the ethical implications of technology use in education.

But let's face it—getting up to speed with digital tools can be daunting, especially for those who didn't grow up with them. This is where professional development comes in. It's not just about teaching educators how to use the latest software; it's about empowering them to rethink how they teach, how they engage with students, and how they can make the most of the digital tools at their disposal. Take Ireland, for example. The country has taken a proactive approach to this challenge through its National Forum for the Enhancement of Teaching and Learning in Higher Education. Since 2013, this initiative has been helping educators across Ireland build their digital competence. One of its most successful programs is the Digital Badge for Online Teaching—a professional development course that's flexible, accessible, and directly relevant to the needs of higher education faculty. What makes this program stand out is its practicality. Educators can complete it online at their own pace, making it easier to fit into their busy schedules. The course covers everything from the basics of online teaching to more advanced topics like creating interactive digital content. And it's not just about ticking a box—educators who complete the program report feeling more confident in their ability to use digital tools in their teaching, which ultimately benefits their students.

Ireland's approach shows that when professional development is tailored to the needs of educators and delivered in a flexible format, it can have a significant impact. It's not just about learning new skills—it's about changing how educators think about teaching in the digital age.

The Challenge of Change

Change is hard, especially when it involves adopting new technologies. Many educators have been teaching for decades and have developed methods that work well for them. Introducing new digital tools can feel like a disruption, and it's natural to resist change, especially if the benefits aren't immediately clear. This resistance isn't just about being stuck in old ways. It's often about fear—fear of the unknown, fear of failure, or fear of not being able to keep up with the rapid pace of technological change. Overcoming this resistance requires more than just offering training sessions; it requires a cultural shift within institutions, one that encourages experimentation, embraces failure as a learning process, and celebrates innovation.

In Japan, the University of Tokyo has recognized this challenge and launched the Digital Teaching Academy in

2022. This initiative was born out of a need to help faculty develop digital skills in a way that felt supportive rather than overwhelming. The Academy offers workshops and courses that start with the basics, gradually building up to more advanced digital teaching techniques. What's interesting about the University of Tokyo's approach is how it addresses the underlying fears that many educators have. The Academy creates a safe space where educators can experiment with digital tools without fear of judgment. They can try out new methods, get feedback from peers, and refine their approach in a supportive environment.

This approach is crucial because it acknowledges that professional development isn't just about acquiring new skills—it's about building confidence and changing mindsets. The University of Tokyo's experience shows that when educators feel supported, they're more likely to embrace digital tools and integrate them into their teaching.

The Ethical Dimension of Digital Competence

As we push for greater digital competence, it's essential to consider the ethical implications. Digital tools offer incredible opportunities, but they also come with risks. Data privacy, cybersecurity, and the potential for technology to exacerbate inequalities are all issues that educators must navigate. When we talk about digital competence, we're not just talking about technical skills—we're talking about the ability to use technology responsibly and ethically. Educators need to understand how to protect student data, how to create inclusive digital environments, and how to use technology in a way that enhances learning without compromising ethical standards.

In Denmark, the University of Copenhagen has taken a leading role in integrating ethics into its professional development programs. Educators are not only taught how to use digital tools but also how to think critically about the ethical implications of their use. This includes understanding data privacy laws, knowing how to protect sensitive information, and being aware of the potential biases that can be built into digital systems. By incorporating ethics into its professional development programs, the University of Copenhagen ensures that educators are not just digitally competent but also ethically aware. This holistic approach to professional development is essential in today's digital age, where the misuse of technology can have serious consequences.

The Impact of Professional Development on Educational Outcomes

So, does professional development in digital competence actually make a difference? The answer, based on numerous studies and examples from around the world, is a resounding yes. When educators are equipped with the right tools and knowledge, they can create learning experiences that are more engaging, effective, and aligned with the needs of today's students.

Singapore's National Institute of Education (NIE) offers a compelling example of how professional development can transform teaching. The NIE's Technology-Enhanced Learning (TEL) program is designed to help educators integrate digital tools into their teaching in a meaningful way. But it's not just about learning to use the tools—it's about rethinking pedagogy in the context of a digital world.

The TEL program encourages educators to experiment, share their experiences with colleagues, and continuously refine their teaching practices. This collaborative, iterative approach has led to significant improvements in student engagement and learning outcomes. A 2023 report by the Singapore Ministry of Education found that students taught by educators who had completed the TEL program were more engaged and achieved better academic results than their peers.

This success underscores the importance of making professional development an ongoing process. Digital competence isn't something that can be learned in a single workshop; it requires continuous learning, experimentation, and adaptation.

The National Digital Library of India (NDLI) is another example of how professional development in digital competence can have a broad impact. The NDLI provides educators with access to a vast array of digital resources, including professional development courses that cover everything from basic computer literacy to advanced online teaching techniques. What's particularly impressive about the NDLI is its reach. By making these resources available online, the NDLI has been able to provide professional development opportunities to educators in remote and underserved areas, who might not otherwise have access to such training. This has not only helped to build digital competence on a large scale but has also contributed to reducing educational inequalities across the country.

India's experience with the NDLI shows that digital platforms can be a powerful tool for expanding access to professional development. By leveraging technology, institutions can ensure that all educators have the opportunity to build the skills they need to succeed, regardless of where they are located.

Looking Ahead

As we look to the future, it's clear that professional development in digital competence will continue to be a priority for higher education institutions around the world. The digital landscape is constantly evolving, and educators need to be equipped to keep up with these changes.

But it's not just about keeping up—it's about leading the way. Educators have the opportunity to be at the forefront of innovation in education, using digital tools to create learning experiences that are more personalized, interactive, and effective. To do this, professional development needs to be ongoing, flexible, and responsive to the changing needs of both educators and students. Emerging technologies like artificial intelligence, virtual reality, and blockchain are already starting to make their way into higher education. These tools offer exciting possibilities for transforming teaching and learning, but they also require new skills and knowledge. Professional development programs will need to evolve to address these emerging technologies, ensuring that educators are prepared to use them in ways that enhance education.

Professional development in digital competence is not just about keeping up with technology—it's about rethinking how we teach, how we engage with students, and how we can create learning experiences that are truly transformative. When educators are equipped with the right skills and support, they can have a profound impact on their students and their institutions. But this journey is not without its challenges. Overcoming resistance to change, addressing ethical concerns, and ensuring that professional development is accessible and relevant are all critical to the success of these initiatives. As we move forward, it's essential that institutions continue to invest in professional development, not as a one-time effort, but as an ongoing process that evolves with the needs of educators and students alike.

In doing so, we can ensure that higher education remains at the cutting edge of innovation, preparing students not just for today's world, but for the challenges and opportunities of the future.

Key Takeaways

- In today's digital age, educators must go beyond traditional teaching methods and embrace digital tools to create more engaging and effective learning experiences. Professional development in digital competence is essential for this transformation.
- Change can be challenging, especially when it involves adopting new technologies. Institutions must create supportive environments that encourage experimentation and build confidence among educators, helping them embrace digital tools without fear.
- Digital competence isn't just about technical skills—it's also about using technology responsibly and ethically. Educators need to understand data privacy, cybersecurity, and the potential impacts of technology on inequality, ensuring they use digital tools in ways that protect and benefit students.

- Professional development in digital competence can lead to significant improvements in student engagement and learning outcomes. Programs that encourage continuous learning and collaboration, like those in Singapore and India, demonstrate the powerful impact that well-supported educators can have.
- As technology continues to evolve, so too must professional development. Institutions need to ensure that educators are equipped not just to keep up with technological changes, but to lead the way in creating innovative, personalized, and effective educational experiences.

Cybersecurity and Data Privacy

"Data is a precious thing and will last longer than the systems themselves. — Tim Berners-Lee"

Imagine a day in the life of a university student. They log into their online classes, submit assignments through a learning management system, and maybe even share personal reflections on a class forum. Behind the scenes, all this activity generates a massive amount of data—grades, personal information, even the research they're working on. Now imagine what happens if that data falls into the wrong hands. It's not just about lost information; it's about trust being shattered, and in the academic world, trust is everything.

In our increasingly digital education landscape, cybersecurity and data privacy aren't just technical concerns—they're fundamental to the integrity of the educational experience. As institutions continue to expand their digital reach, the risks associated with cyber threats grow in parallel. This chapter explores the challenges educational institutions face in safeguarding sensitive data and examines how they can implement robust cybersecurity measures to protect their communities. Through examples from around the world, we'll see how different institutions are tackling these issues and what lessons we can learn from their experiences.

The Reality of Cybersecurity Threats in Education

Let's start with a reality check: educational institutions are prime targets for cybercriminals. Why? Because they hold vast amounts of valuable data, from student records and financial information to cutting-edge research. And unlike corporations that often have centralized security systems, universities and colleges tend to be more decentralized, which can create vulnerabilities.

Consider what happened to the University of California, San Francisco (UCSF) in 2023. UCSF was hit by a ransomware attack that encrypted vital data, essentially locking it away until a ransom was paid. Despite having solid cybersecurity measures in place, the attackers found and exploited a vulnerability. The result? UCSF had to pay a significant ransom to regain access to its data. This incident was a wake-up call for many in the higher education sector. It underscored a hard truth: no matter how prepared you think you are, cybercriminals are constantly evolving, finding new ways to infiltrate systems. UCSF's Chief Information Officer put it well when he said, "Cybersecurity is not a one-time effort—it requires ongoing commitment, investment, and adaptation to evolving threats." This is a crucial point—cybersecurity isn't something you can set and forget. It requires constant vigilance, and that's something every institution needs to understand.

The Challenges of Protecting Sensitive Data

Educational institutions face unique challenges when it comes to protecting sensitive data. Unlike businesses, which often operate in a more controlled environment, universities are open by design. They thrive on collaboration and the free exchange of ideas, which is fantastic for education but can be a nightmare for cybersecurity.

Take the University of Warwick in the UK as an example. In 2024, Warwick experienced a data breach that exposed personal information about students and staff. The breach happened because of a phishing attack—a deceptive email tricked university employees into handing over their login credentials. Once the attackers had access, they were able to get into the system and steal sensitive data, including names, addresses, and even financial details. What happened at Warwick highlights a critical challenge: even the best security systems can be compromised by human error. This is why cybersecurity training and awareness are so important. After the breach, Warwick launched mandatory cybersecurity training for all staff, not just those in IT. The goal was to create a culture where everyone is aware of the risks and knows how to protect themselves and the institution from potential threats. This example from Warwick shows that technology alone isn't enough. You need to have the people using that technology on board as well, educated about the risks and their role in keeping data safe.

Building Strong Cybersecurity Measures

So, how can educational institutions build strong cybersecurity defenses? It's not just about having the latest technology—it's about a comprehensive approach that includes policies, procedures, and, crucially, people.

South Korea provides a compelling example of what a coordinated approach to cybersecurity can look like. In 2022, the South Korean government, recognizing the growing threat of cyberattacks, launched a National Cybersecurity Strategy specifically for universities. This strategy isn't just about protecting individual institutions—it's about creating a unified front against cyber threats. Under this strategy, universities are required to follow a centralized cybersecurity framework, which includes regular security audits, the establishment of incident response teams, and the deployment of advanced threat detection systems. But it's not just about the technology—there's also a strong emphasis on training. Students, faculty, and staff all receive ongoing cybersecurity education to ensure they're aware of the latest threats and how to avoid them. What's particularly effective about South Korea's approach is the emphasis on collaboration. By standardizing cybersecurity practices across the country's universities, they've managed to raise the overall security level, making it harder for cybercriminals to find weaknesses to exploit.

This approach shows the power of working together—when institutions don't have to face cyber threats alone, they can share resources, knowledge, and strategies to stay ahead of the curve.

The Role of Data Privacy in Education

While cybersecurity is about keeping systems safe from attacks, data privacy is about how we handle the information we collect. In the context of education, this is particularly sensitive. Universities and colleges handle a lot of personal data—everything from student grades to research data—and they have a responsibility to protect that information.

One of the most significant developments in data privacy in recent years has been the General Data Protection Regulation (GDPR) in Europe. GDPR, which came into effect in 2018, set a high bar for how personal data must be handled, with strict rules about obtaining consent, storing data securely, and the rights of individuals to access and delete their data. For European universities, GDPR has been a game-changer. It has required them to rethink how they manage data at every level. For instance, universities must now obtain explicit consent from students and staff before collecting their data, and they must ensure that this data is stored securely and only used for its intended purpose. One challenge that has emerged under GDPR is balancing the need for data privacy with the requirements of academic research. Research often involves large datasets, and GDPR's restrictions can make it difficult to work with this data. To address this, many universities have established Data Protection Offices, which work closely with researchers to ensure that their work complies with GDPR while still enabling valuable research to continue.

GDPR has also pushed universities to invest in better data management systems, including encryption and access controls. These systems help protect data throughout its lifecycle, ensuring that it's secure from the moment it's collected until it's no longer needed.

Creating a Culture of Cybersecurity and Data Privacy

At the end of the day, the most sophisticated technology and the strictest policies won't protect an institution if the people within it aren't on board. Creating a culture of cybersecurity and data privacy is crucial. This means making sure that everyone—students, faculty, and staff—understands the importance of protecting data and knows how to do it.

The University of Queensland in Australia has taken an innovative approach to building this kind of culture. In 2023, the university launched a Cybersecurity Awareness Initiative designed to make cybersecurity a part of everyday life on campus. This initiative includes mandatory training for all staff and students, regular phishing simulations to test how well people can spot suspicious emails, and a communications campaign that keeps cybersecurity top of mind. But what really sets Queensland's approach apart is its emphasis on making cybersecurity relatable. The training uses real-world scenarios to show the potential impact of cybersecurity breaches, making the risks feel personal rather than abstract. The university also provides practical resources, like tips for creating strong passwords and advice on how to secure personal devices, making it easy for everyone to take action. Since launching the initiative, the University of Queensland has seen a noticeable drop in successful phishing attacks and an increase in overall cybersecurity awareness. This shows that when cybersecurity is presented in a way that connects with people's everyday experiences, it's much more likely to stick.

The Indian Institute of Technology (IIT) Bombay has also recognized the importance of creating a culture around data privacy. In 2024, IIT Bombay launched a Data Privacy Initiative aimed at educating both students and staff about their rights and responsibilities regarding data protection. This initiative includes workshops that cover everything from understanding data privacy laws to best practices for handling personal information. IIT Bombay has also implemented a comprehensive data privacy policy that outlines how personal data is collected, stored, and used within the institution. What's powerful about IIT Bombay's approach is its focus on empowerment. By educating the university community about data privacy, they're not just protecting the institution—they're also giving individuals the knowledge they need to protect themselves in an increasingly digital world.

The Evolving Landscape of Cybersecurity and Data Privacy

As technology continues to advance, the challenges of cybersecurity and data privacy in education will only grow. Emerging technologies like artificial intelligence, blockchain, and quantum computing offer new ways to secure data, but they also introduce new risks. Educational institutions must remain vigilant, continuously updating their cybersecurity measures and adapting to new threats. One area that's likely to see significant growth in the coming years is the integration of cybersecurity and data privacy education into university curricula. By teaching students about these issues early on, universities can help build a generation that's not only digitally literate but also deeply aware of the importance of protecting personal information.

In Finland, universities are already taking steps in this direction. The University of Helsinki, for instance, launched a Cybersecurity and Data Privacy course in 2024, designed for students across all disciplines. The course covers everything from basic cybersecurity practices to the ethical implications of data privacy, helping students understand the critical role these issues play in the digital world. By integrating cybersecurity and data privacy into the curriculum, Finnish universities are ensuring that all students—not just those studying IT—are equipped with the knowledge they need to navigate the digital landscape safely and responsibly. This approach not only enhances the individual's understanding but also contributes to a broader culture of cybersecurity and data privacy within the institution.

Cybersecurity and data privacy are more than just technical challenges for educational institutions—they're fundamental to the trust and integrity that underpin the educational experience. These challenges are complex and global, requiring a coordinated, multi-faceted approach. Institutions must invest not only in the latest technologies and policies but also in their people, creating a culture where cybersecurity and data privacy are everyone's responsibility. As technology continues to evolve, so too must our efforts to protect the sensitive information entrusted to educational institutions.

By staying vigilant, fostering a culture of awareness, and continuously adapting to new threats, educational institutions can safeguard their digital environments, protect their communities, and maintain the trust that is so crucial to their mission. The future of education depends on our ability to secure the digital foundations upon which it increasingly relies.

Key Takeaways

- Educational institutions are prime targets for cybercriminals due to the vast amounts of valuable data they hold. The increasing sophistication of cyberattacks, as seen in cases like UCSF, underscores the need for continuous vigilance and investment in cybersecurity.
- Even the most advanced security systems can be compromised by human error, as highlighted by the data breach at Warwick University. Building a culture of cybersecurity awareness among staff, students, and faculty is crucial to protecting sensitive data.
- South Korea's National Cybersecurity Strategy for Universities demonstrates the effectiveness of a coordinated, standardized approach to cybersecurity. By working together, institutions can raise the overall security level and better defend against cyber threats.
- The implementation of GDPR has shown how data privacy regulations can drive significant changes in how universities manage and protect personal information. Balancing privacy with the needs of academic research requires careful planning and robust data management practices.
- Technology and policies alone are not enough; fostering a culture where cybersecurity and data privacy are everyone's responsibility is essential. Initiatives like those at the University of Queensland and IIT Bombay illustrate the power of education and communication in building this culture.

CHAPTER XII

E-Learning and Distance Education

"Learning never exhausts the mind. — Leonardo da Vinci"

The landscape of education has undergone a profound transformation in recent years, with e-learning and distance education emerging as powerful modalities that are reshaping how knowledge is delivered and acquired. What was once considered a niche alternative to traditional classroom-based learning has now become a mainstream approach, embraced by institutions and learners across the globe. The rapid advancement of technology, coupled with changing societal needs, has driven this shift, creating both opportunities and challenges for educational leaders.

In this chapter, we'll take a journey through the rise of e-learning and distance education. We'll explore how these modalities have evolved, the hurdles they present, and the exciting possibilities they offer for the future of education. Along the way, we'll look at real-world examples from around the globe, offering insights into how different institutions are embracing this change and what it means for educators and students alike.

The Evolution of E-Learning and Distance Education

E-learning and distance education have come a long way from their humble beginnings. What started as correspondence courses delivered by mail has now blossomed into a sophisticated system of online learning platforms, video lectures, and interactive content. The COVID-19 pandemic acted as a catalyst, pushing educational institutions worldwide to adopt online learning on a scale never seen before. But now, as we settle into this new normal, we see that e-learning is not just a temporary fix—it's here to stay.

Let's take a look at Indira Gandhi National Open University (IGNOU) in India, which has been a trailblazer in distance education for decades. In 2024, IGNOU launched a new e-learning platform that uses AI to create personalized learning experiences for its diverse student population. Whether you're a working professional, a homemaker, or someone living in a remote village, IGNOU's platform adapts to your needs, making learning more accessible than ever. Dr. Nageshwar Rao, Vice-Chancellor of IGNOU, shared his vision: "Education should be a right, not a privilege. With our new platform, we're breaking down barriers and making sure that everyone has the opportunity to learn, no matter where they are."

IGNOU's commitment to making education accessible to all is a perfect example of how e-learning can democratize education, offering opportunities to those who might otherwise be left behind.

The Challenges of E-Learning and Distance Education

While the rise of e-learning has opened up new possibilities, it hasn't been without its challenges. Educational leaders must address these issues to ensure that online learning is not only effective but also equitable and sustainable.

Bridging the Digital Divide

One of the biggest challenges is the digital divide. Not everyone has access to the high-speed internet, devices, or even the quiet space needed to participate in online learning. This gap can widen existing inequalities, leaving some students struggling to keep up.

The University of the Philippines Open University (UPOU) has been proactive in addressing this issue. In 2024, they launched an initiative to provide students in remote areas with affordable tablets and data plans, ensuring that they can access online classes. They also developed offline learning materials that students could use without needing an internet connection. Dr. Melinda Bandalaria, Chancellor of UPOU, emphasized the importance of inclusivity: "E-learning shouldn't be a luxury. By providing the necessary tools and resources, we're making sure that every student, regardless of their circumstances, has the opportunity to learn."

UPOU's approach is a reminder that for e-learning to be truly effective, it must be accessible to everyone, not just those who can afford it.

Keeping Students Engaged and Motivated

Another challenge is keeping students engaged and motivated in an online environment. Without the physical presence of a classroom and the immediate interaction with peers and instructors, some students find it difficult to stay focused and motivated.

The Open University in the UK has long been a leader in distance education, and they've been tackling this issue head-on. In 2024, they introduced AI-driven tools that track student progress and provide personalized feedback, helping students stay on track. They also revamped their online forums to create a more interactive and supportive community for their learners. Professor Mary Kellett, Vice-Chancellor of The Open University, spoke about their approach: "Learning can be a lonely journey, especially online. By using technology to provide personalized support and foster a sense of community, we're helping our students stay engaged and achieve their goals."

The Open University's focus on engagement shows that with the right strategies, online learning can be just as engaging and supportive as traditional classroom education.

Ensuring Quality and Integrity

Maintaining the quality of education and upholding academic integrity in an online setting presents another challenge. With assessments conducted remotely, concerns about cheating and plagiarism are heightened, and the variability in the quality of online courses can be a concern.

The University of Southern Queensland (USQ) has addressed these concerns by implementing a robust quality assurance process for its online courses. In 2024, they introduced AI tools to monitor course content and ensure it meets the university's high standards. They also implemented advanced plagiarism detection software and online proctoring systems to maintain academic integrity during exams. Dr. Geraldine Mackenzie, Vice-Chancellor of USQ, stressed the importance of quality: "Online education should be held to the same standards as traditional education. By using the latest technology, we're ensuring that our online courses are rigorous, credible, and respected by employers and academics alike."

USQ's efforts highlight the importance of maintaining high standards in e-learning, ensuring that online education is both credible and valuable.

The Opportunities of E-Learning and Distance Education

Despite the challenges, e-learning and distance education offer exciting opportunities for educational leaders to innovate and expand access to education in ways that were previously unimaginable.

Expanding Access to a Global Audience

One of the most significant opportunities is the ability to reach students worldwide. E-learning breaks down geographical barriers, allowing students from different countries and backgrounds to learn together, enriching the educational experience for everyone.

The University of Edinburgh has embraced this opportunity by offering a wide range of online master's programs designed for a global audience. In 2024, they launched new programs in fields like data science and digital health, attracting students from around the world who might not have had the opportunity to study at Edinburgh otherwise. Professor Peter Mathieson, Principal and Vice-Chancellor of the University of Edinburgh, reflected on the impact: "Our online programs are creating a global classroom, where students from diverse backgrounds come together to learn and grow. This not only enriches the learning experience but also prepares our students to thrive in an interconnected world."

The University of Edinburgh's success shows how e-learning can expand access to education, creating opportunities for students worldwide.

Innovating in Teaching and Learning

E-learning also opens the door to new ways of teaching and learning. With digital tools, educators can experiment with innovative approaches like flipped classrooms, gamification, and personalized learning paths that cater to individual student needs.

Nanyang Technological University (NTU) has been a leader in educational innovation, particularly in the online space. In 2024, NTU launched "NTU Learn+," a platform that uses AI to tailor the learning experience to each student. The platform also incorporates gamification elements to make learning more engaging and enjoyable. Professor Subra Suresh, President of NTU, explained the vision: "With NTU Learn+, we're rethinking how education is delivered. By leveraging AI and gamification, we're creating a learning experience that's not only effective but also exciting for our students."

NTU's approach illustrates how e-learning can be used to innovate and improve the educational experience, making it more dynamic and responsive to student needs.

Supporting Lifelong Learning and Professional Development

In today's fast-paced world, the need for lifelong learning and continuous professional development has never been greater. E-learning offers a flexible and convenient way for individuals to update their skills and stay competitive in the job market.

The University of Helsinki has embraced e-learning as a key component of its lifelong learning strategy. In 2024, the university launched a series of online courses designed for working professionals in fields such as digital marketing and environmental science. These courses are short, focused, and can be completed at the learner's own pace, making them ideal for busy professionals. Professor Sari Lindblom, Rector of the University of Helsinki, emphasized the importance of lifelong learning: "Learning doesn't stop when you graduate. Our online courses are designed to help professionals stay ahead in their careers, providing them with the skills they need to succeed in a rapidly changing world."

The University of Helsinki's focus on lifelong learning shows how e-learning can support continuous education, offering individuals the flexibility and access they need to keep learning throughout their lives.

E-learning and distance education have transformed the educational landscape, offering both challenges and opportunities for institutions around the world. While the transition to online learning has not been without its difficulties, it has also opened up new possibilities for expanding access, innovating in teaching and learning, and supporting lifelong education. Educational leaders are finding creative and effective ways to navigate these challenges and make the most of the opportunities presented by e-learning. By staying flexible, forward-thinking, and committed to inclusivity and quality, institutions can harness the power of e-learning to create a brighter future for education.

As we look to the future, it's clear that e-learning and distance education will continue to play a vital role in the global education system. The lessons learned from these institutions can serve as a guide for educational leaders as they navigate this evolving landscape, ensuring that online learning remains a powerful and positive force in education.

Key Takeaways

- E-learning has the power to break down barriers, making education accessible to a broader audience, regardless of geography or socio-economic status. Institutions like IGNOU demonstrate how technology can be used to reach students who might otherwise be left behind.
- While e-learning offers many opportunities, it also highlights existing inequalities. Ensuring that all students have access to the necessary technology and resources is essential for making online education equitable, as seen in UPOU's efforts to provide affordable tablets and offline materials.
- Keeping students engaged in a virtual environment requires thoughtful strategies and the use of technology to personalize the learning experience. The Open University's use of AI to track progress and create interactive communities showcases how institutions can

keep students motivated online.

- Maintaining the quality and integrity of education in an online setting is crucial. Universities like USQ have implemented rigorous quality assurance processes and advanced tools to ensure that their online courses are as credible and valuable as traditional education.
- In a rapidly changing world, e-learning provides a flexible and accessible way for individuals to continue learning throughout their lives. The University of Helsinki's focus on lifelong learning shows how online education can help professionals stay competitive and up-to-date with industry trends.

CHAPTER XIII

Leadership in Times of Crisis

"In times of crisis, the wise build bridges while the foolish build barriers. — African Proverb"

The COVID-19 pandemic was a time that none of us will forget. It shook the foundations of our lives and forced us to rethink almost everything, including how we educate. As classrooms emptied and campuses closed, educational leaders faced challenges that were unimaginable just a few months before. The crisis demanded more than just quick decisions—it required empathy, resilience, and a deep commitment to the well-being of students and staff.

In this chapter, we'll explore how the pandemic reshaped educational leadership, not just in terms of strategy but in the way leaders connect with their communities. We'll reflect on the lessons learned and the lasting changes that have come out of this period, using real-world examples that show how institutions around the world adapted, innovated, and ultimately, grew stronger.

The Initial Shock

When the pandemic first hit, it felt like the ground was shifting beneath our feet. Schools and universities had to pivot overnight, moving from in-person instruction to online platforms. For many leaders, this was a moment of intense pressure—how do you keep an institution running when the world outside is falling apart?

At the University of Cape Town (UCT), the sudden switch to online learning was a massive challenge, especially given the socio-economic diversity of the student body. Many students didn't have access to the necessary technology or reliable internet connections at home. Vice-Chancellor Mamokgethi Phakeng and her team quickly mobilized to address these issues, partnering with local telecom companies to provide students with free or subsidized data. They also worked to ensure that all students had access to devices, setting up a loan program for those in need. Dr. Phakeng shared her thoughts on that time: "It wasn't just about moving classes online—it was about making sure that every single student had the chance to continue their education, despite everything that was happening. We had to think on our feet, and we had to act fast."

UCT's experience shows that during a crisis, leaders need to be both quick and compassionate, making decisions that consider the diverse needs of their community.

Adapting to a New Reality

As the pandemic dragged on, it became clear that the changes it brought weren't just temporary. Educational leaders had to shift from short-term crisis management to developing strategies that could sustain their institutions through the long haul. This wasn't just about keeping the lights on—it was about rethinking what education could and should look like in a world where uncertainty had become the norm.

The National University of Singapore (NUS) took this opportunity to accelerate its digital transformation. Realizing that a blend of online and in-person learning would likely be the future, NUS invested heavily in technology and digital resources. They launched the "NUS Resilience Initiative," which aimed to create a flexible, robust digital ecosystem capable of supporting both synchronous and asynchronous learning. Professor Tan Eng Chye, President of NUS, explained their approach: "The pandemic made it clear that we needed to be more adaptable. By investing in our digital infrastructure, we've positioned ourselves not just to survive the current crisis, but to thrive in the future."

NUS's proactive approach highlights a key lesson: crises can be catalysts for long-term, positive change. Leaders who are willing to adapt and invest in the future will be better equipped to handle whatever comes next.

The Human Connection

One of the most profound challenges of the pandemic was the impact it had on mental health. The isolation, uncertainty, and constant stress took a toll on students, staff, and leaders alike. Educational leaders found themselves not only managing logistics but also caring for the emotional and psychological well-being of their communities.

The University of Melbourne recognized early on that mental health would be a significant issue during the pandemic. Vice-Chancellor Duncan Maskell and his team launched a comprehensive mental health support program that included online counseling, virtual wellness workshops, and regular check-ins with students and staff. They even introduced a "Wellness Week," encouraging everyone to step back, take a breath, and focus on self-care. Vice-Chancellor Maskell reflected on the importance of this initiative: "We knew that people were struggling, and it was essential that we provided more than just academic support. We needed to let our students and staff know that we were there for them, no matter what."

The University of Melbourne's approach reminds us that leadership during a crisis isn't just about maintaining operations—it's about caring for the people who make up the institution.

Innovating in Crisis

While the pandemic brought many challenges, it also opened the door to innovation. Educational leaders who embraced this moment as an opportunity to try new things found themselves not only navigating the crisis but also paving the way for future success.

At Universidad de los Andes in Colombia, the shift to online learning was seen as an opportunity to innovate. Rector Alejandro Gaviria and his team introduced a range of new initiatives, including interactive virtual classrooms, partnerships with tech companies to provide cutting-edge educational tools, and the creation of online courses tailored to the needs of students during the pandemic. Rector Gaviria shared his perspective: "The pandemic forced us to think differently about education. It was challenging, yes, but it also allowed us to experiment and grow. We've developed new tools and approaches that will continue to benefit our students long after the pandemic is over."

The experience of Universidad de los Andes shows that even in the midst of a crisis, there are opportunities to innovate and improve. Leaders who are open to change can turn challenges into strengths.

The Legacy of the Pandemic

As we begin to move beyond the immediate impacts of the COVID-19 pandemic, it's clear that the lessons learned during this time will leave a lasting legacy. The crisis has reshaped how educational leaders think about everything from crisis management to digital transformation to mental health.

The University of Oxford, known for its long-standing traditions, found itself at the forefront of educational innovation during the pandemic. Under the leadership of Vice-Chancellor Louise Richardson, the university implemented significant changes that have transformed how education is delivered at Oxford. These changes include integrating online learning into traditional courses, developing new digital assessment methods, and enhancing global collaboration and research efforts. Vice-Chancellor Richardson reflected on the long-term impact of the pandemic: "The challenges we faced during the pandemic pushed us to innovate in ways we hadn't anticipated. The changes we've made will continue to shape the future of education at Oxford, ensuring that we remain at the forefront of global academic leadership."

Oxford's experience highlights the enduring impact of the pandemic on educational leadership. The crisis has spurred innovation, adaptation, and a renewed focus on resilience and flexibility.

The COVID-19 pandemic was a defining moment for educational leaders around the world. It tested their resilience, adaptability, and empathy in ways that few could have predicted. Effective leadership during this crisis required a blend of quick thinking, long-term planning, and deep compassion for the people involved.

The lessons learned from the pandemic will continue to guide educational leaders as they face future challenges. The importance of being adaptable, investing in digital infrastructure, supporting mental health, and finding opportunities for innovation will remain critical. As we move forward, these experiences will help shape a more resilient, flexible, and compassionate approach to educational leadership, ensuring that institutions are better prepared for whatever the future holds.

Key Takeaways

- The COVID-19 pandemic highlighted the need for educational leaders to make swift, informed decisions to ensure continuity and support for their communities, as seen in the University of Cape Town's rapid response to student needs.
- Successful leadership during the pandemic involved not just short-term fixes but also long-term strategies, like the National University of Singapore's investment in digital infrastructure, which positioned institutions to thrive in an uncertain future.
- The crisis underscored the importance of addressing the mental and emotional well-being of students and staff. The University of Melbourne's focus on mental health initiatives reminds us that caring for the people within an institution is as important as maintaining its operations.
- Leaders who embraced the challenges of the pandemic as opportunities to innovate, such as Universidad de los Andes, demonstrated that crises can be a catalyst

for positive change, paving the way for new tools and approaches that benefit the institution long-term.

- The COVID-19 pandemic has left a lasting impact on educational leadership, pushing leaders to rethink traditional approaches and embrace flexibility, resilience, and a commitment to the well-being of their communities, ensuring they are better prepared for future challenges.

CHAPTER XIV

Global Trends in Education

"The world is a book, and those who do not travel read only one page. — Saint Augustine"

In a world that feels increasingly connected, education has become a truly global endeavor. Gone are the days when learning was confined to local classrooms or national borders. Today, ideas, knowledge, and students flow freely across continents, creating a rich tapestry of educational experiences. But with this global interconnection comes a host of challenges and opportunities that educational leaders must navigate. How do we embrace the benefits of globalization while maintaining the unique identities of our institutions? How do we prepare students to thrive in a world that's constantly evolving?

In this chapter, we'll dive into the global trends that are shaping education today. We'll explore how institutions are collaborating across borders, how technology is transforming the way we learn, and what it means to lead in this new, interconnected world. Along the way, we'll share stories from around the globe, offering insights that resonate on both an intellectual and emotional level.

A World Without Borders

Imagine a classroom where students from different corners of the globe come together to discuss ideas, share perspectives, and learn from each other's cultures. This is the reality of today's globalized education. As our world becomes more interconnected, the boundaries that once separated educational institutions are fading. Students are no longer limited to the opportunities within their own countries—they can now access resources, expertise, and networks from around the world.

Take Jawaharlal Nehru University (JNU) in India, for instance. JNU has long recognized the importance of thinking beyond its borders. By forging partnerships with universities in Asia, Europe, and North America, JNU has created a global network that benefits both students and faculty. These collaborations have led to joint degree programs, research initiatives, and student exchanges that provide a richer, more diverse educational experience. Dr. Santishree Pandit, Vice-Chancellor of JNU, reflected on the impact of these partnerships: "In today's world, education cannot be insular. Our students need to be exposed to a variety of perspectives and ideas. By collaborating internationally, we're preparing them to be global citizens who can navigate and contribute to an interconnected world."

This approach highlights a key lesson for educational leaders: embracing globalization doesn't mean losing your institution's identity. Instead, it's about enriching that identity by engaging with the broader global community.

Building Bridges Across Borders

One of the most exciting aspects of globalized education is the opportunity for international collaboration. Universities and colleges are increasingly working together across borders to share resources, enhance learning, and tackle some of the world's most pressing challenges. These collaborations are more than just academic exchanges—they're about building lasting relationships that foster mutual understanding and respect.

Consider the partnership between the University of Cape Town (UCT) in South Africa and Humboldt University of Berlin in Germany. This collaboration goes beyond traditional academic exchanges. Together, these universities are tackling climate change and its impact on urban environments—a challenge that requires a global perspective. Through joint research, faculty exchanges, and a shared curriculum, students from both institutions are learning to address real-world problems with a global mindset. Professor Mamokgethi Phakeng, Vice-Chancellor of UCT, shared her thoughts on the value of this partnership: "Collaborating with Humboldt University has not only strengthened our research but has also given our students a chance to learn in a truly global context. It's these kinds of partnerships that prepare our students to become leaders in a world that's more interconnected than ever."

This example underscores the power of international collaboration in education. When institutions work together, they create opportunities for learning that go far beyond the classroom, helping students develop the skills and perspectives they need to succeed in a globalized world.

Connecting the World

Technology has been a game-changer in global education. The rise of online learning platforms, virtual classrooms, and digital communication tools has made it easier than ever for students and educators to connect across continents. This technological revolution has opened up new possibilities for collaboration, allowing institutions to offer joint courses, share resources, and create learning experiences that transcend geographical boundaries.

The University of Tokyo has embraced this potential with its "Global Classroom" initiative. Launched in 2024, this program allows students from around the world to participate in courses taught by Tokyo's faculty. Using state-of-the-art technology, the Global Classroom creates an immersive, interactive learning environment where students can engage with each other and with instructors, no matter where they are. Professor Makoto Gonokami, President of the University of Tokyo, explained the vision behind the initiative: "We believe that education should not be limited by geography. With the Global Classroom, we're creating a space where students and educators from different parts of the world can come together to learn, share ideas, and build a global community of scholars."

The Global Classroom is a powerful reminder of how technology can break down barriers and create new opportunities for learning. For educational leaders, it's a call to explore how digital tools can enhance the global reach of their institutions.

Embracing Global Perspectives

As the world becomes more interconnected, there's a growing recognition that education must prepare students to thrive in a global society. This has led to significant changes in curriculum and pedagogy, with a focus on incorporating global perspectives, fostering cross-cultural understanding, and promoting interdisciplinary approaches. These shifts are helping to create more inclusive, diverse educational experiences that reflect the realities of our interconnected world.

Ashesi University in Ghana is a shining example of how an institution can embrace a global perspective while staying true to its local roots. The university's curriculum is designed to prepare students for leadership roles both in Africa and on the global stage. Courses emphasize ethical leadership, entrepreneurship, and cross-cultural understanding, giving students the tools they need to navigate a complex, interconnected world. Dr. Patrick Awuah, Founder and President of Ashesi University, articulated the university's philosophy: "Our goal is to create leaders who are not only grounded in their own cultures but also have the knowledge and skills to operate in a global context. We believe that a global perspective is essential for addressing the challenges of the 21st century."

Ashesi University's approach highlights the importance of preparing students to think globally while acting locally. By incorporating global perspectives into the curriculum, educational leaders can equip their students with the skills and knowledge they need to succeed in an interconnected world.

Navigating the Challenges of Globalization

While globalization offers many opportunities, it also brings challenges that educational leaders must navigate. Cultural differences, language barriers, and varying educational standards can complicate international collaborations. Additionally, there's the risk of cultural homogenization, where the unique identities of institutions and communities may be overshadowed by dominant global trends.

Tsinghua University in China has been mindful of these challenges as it expands its international collaborations. The university has developed strategies to ensure that its partnerships respect and preserve the cultural identities of all parties involved. For example, Tsinghua has established guidelines for cross-cultural communication and collaboration, ensuring that cultural sensitivity is a key component of all international projects. Professor Qiu Yong, President of Tsinghua University, emphasized the importance of balancing global engagement with cultural preservation: "As we engage with partners around the world, it's crucial that we maintain a balance between embracing global perspectives and preserving our own cultural heritage. This balance is what makes our collaborations truly meaningful and sustainable."

Tsinghua University's approach illustrates that successful navigation of globalization's challenges requires a deep understanding of cultural differences and a commitment to preserving the unique identities of all involved. Educational leaders must be mindful of these challenges to ensure that their institutions remain culturally rich and diverse.

The Evolving Role of Educational Leaders

In this globalized world, the role of educational leaders has become more complex and demanding. Leaders must not only manage their institutions but also navigate the intricacies of international collaboration, cultural exchange, and global competition. This requires a new set of skills—leaders must be able to think globally while acting locally, fostering an environment where both global and local perspectives are valued and integrated.

The University of Sydney has recognized the need for global leadership in education and has developed a Global Leadership Program for its faculty and administrators. This program includes training in cross-cultural communication, international collaboration, and global strategic planning. It's designed to equip leaders with the tools they need to navigate the complexities of globalization and lead their institutions successfully on the global stage. Professor Mark Scott, Vice-Chancellor of the University of Sydney, shared his thoughts on the importance of global leadership: "In today's interconnected world, educational leaders need to be global thinkers. Our Global Leadership Program is about preparing our leaders to not only understand global trends but to actively shape them in ways that benefit our institution and our broader community."

The University of Sydney's focus on global leadership development underscores the importance of equipping educational leaders with the skills and knowledge they need to navigate a rapidly changing world. As globalization continues to reshape education, the ability to lead effectively in a global context will be a critical component of successful educational leadership.

The world of education is evolving rapidly, driven by the forces of globalization, technology, and cross-cultural exchange. As educational leaders, it's essential to embrace these changes while remaining true to the unique identities of our institutions. By fostering international collaborations, leveraging technology, and incorporating global perspectives into our curricula, we can prepare our students to thrive in an interconnected world. Global engagement is not just about reaching out—it's about building meaningful, sustainable partnerships that enrich our institutions and empower our students.

As we move forward, the role of educational leaders will be to navigate this complex, global landscape with vision, empathy, and a commitment to excellence. By doing so, we can ensure that our institutions not only survive but thrive in this new era of global education, creating opportunities for learning that are as diverse and dynamic as the world we live in.

Key Takeaways

- Embracing globalization allows educational institutions to engage in international collaborations that enhance learning, research, and cultural exchange, preparing students to become global citizens.
- The rise of digital tools and online platforms has made global education more accessible, creating opportunities for students and educators to connect and learn from one another, regardless of location.
- While globalization offers many benefits, it's essential to balance global engagement with the preservation of cultural identities. Successful international collaborations respect and integrate diverse cultural perspectives.
- To prepare students for the complexities of a globalized world, educational leaders should integrate global perspectives and cross-cultural understanding into their curricula, fostering a more inclusive and holistic educational experience.
- Educational leaders must develop the ability to think globally while acting locally, navigating the complexities of international collaboration and global trends to guide

their institutions effectively in a rapidly changing world.

122

Building a Culture of Innovation

"Innovation distinguishes between a leader and a follower. — Steve Jobs"

Innovation is the heartbeat of progress, and nowhere is this more important than in education. As the world around us rapidly evolves, educational institutions face the challenge—and the opportunity—of adapting to these changes. The question is, how do we foster a culture of innovation within our schools and universities? How do we create environments where creativity thrives, where new ideas are not only welcomed but celebrated, and where the fear of failure is overshadowed by the excitement of discovery?

In this chapter, we'll explore how educational leaders can cultivate a culture of innovation. We'll dive into stories from around the world, looking at how different institutions are pushing boundaries and reimagining what education can be. Through these examples, we'll see how fostering a spirit of experimentation, adopting new technologies, and embracing continuous learning can transform educational institutions into dynamic hubs of innovation.

The Necessity of Innovation in Education

We live in a time of extraordinary change. Technology is advancing at a breakneck pace, the job market is constantly shifting, and students' needs are more diverse than ever. In this context, standing still is not an option. Educational institutions must innovate if they are to remain relevant and effective in preparing students for the future.

Let's start with Amity University in India, a place that has made innovation a core part of its DNA. Recognizing the need to stay ahead, Amity has embraced new technologies like artificial intelligence, virtual reality, and blockchain to enhance the learning experience. But innovation at Amity isn't just about using the latest gadgets. It's about rethinking education itself. The university has introduced flexible learning models that allow students to tailor their education to fit their lives, whether they're working professionals, full-time students, or somewhere in between. Dr. Ashok Chauhan, Founder and President of Amity University, often speaks about the importance of challenging the status quo: "Innovation is about more than just technology. It's about asking, 'How can we do this better? How can we make learning more effective, more engaging, more accessible?' At Amity, we're constantly looking for new ways to improve the student experience because we believe that's what will prepare our students for the future."

Amity's approach shows us that innovation isn't a one-size-fits-all solution. It's about creating a mindset—a culture—where new ideas can flourish and where the focus is always on how to improve.

Creating a Safe Space for Experimentation

One of the biggest barriers to innovation is the fear of failure. In many educational institutions, there's a tendency to stick with what's safe, what's known. But innovation requires risk-taking. It requires an environment where faculty, staff, and students feel empowered to try new things, even if they don't always succeed.

Stanford University is a place where experimentation is in the air. Known for its innovative spirit, Stanford has created an environment where risk-taking is not only accepted but encouraged. The d.school (Hasso Plattner Institute of Design) is a perfect example of this. Here, students from diverse disciplines come together to tackle real-world problems using design thinking—a process that values ideation, prototyping, and iteration. It's a place where failing is just another step toward finding the right solution. Professor Sarah Stein Greenberg, Executive Director of the d.school, puts it this way: "Innovation happens when people feel safe to explore the unknown. At Stanford, we've built a culture where students and faculty can push the boundaries of their creativity without fear. We believe that some of the best ideas come from taking risks and learning from what doesn't work."

Stanford's approach teaches us that for innovation to thrive, educational leaders must create safe spaces for experimentation. It's about fostering a culture where trying something new is celebrated, even if it doesn't work out the first time.

Integrating Technology Thoughtfully

When we think of innovation, technology often comes to mind. But simply adopting the latest tech isn't enough. The key is to integrate technology in a way that enhances the educational experience—where it becomes a tool for deeper learning rather than a distraction.

Nanyang Technological University (NTU) in Singapore has mastered the art of integrating technology into education. NTU has introduced a range of innovative technologies, including AI-powered learning platforms, virtual laboratories, and interactive digital classrooms. But what sets NTU apart is how these technologies are woven into the fabric of the university's curriculum. They're not just add-ons; they're central to how learning happens. Professor Subra Suresh, President of NTU, explains: "Technology should serve the mission of education, not the other way around. At NTU, we use technology to make learning more interactive, more personalized, and more engaging. But we're always careful to ensure that the tools we adopt enhance the learning experience rather than detract from it."

NTU's approach reminds us that technology is a means to an end, not an end in itself. Educational leaders must be thoughtful in how they integrate new tools, ensuring they align with the institution's broader educational goals.

Fostering Collaboration and Inclusivity

Innovation doesn't happen in a vacuum. It thrives in environments where diverse perspectives come together, where collaboration and inclusivity are prioritized. Educational leaders must create spaces where faculty, staff, and students from different backgrounds can collaborate, share ideas, and work together to solve complex problems.

The University of Cape Town (UCT) has made collaboration and inclusivity the cornerstones of its innovation strategy. UCT's "Innovation Hub" is a space where students, faculty, and industry partners collaborate on projects that address real-world challenges. What's unique about the Innovation Hub is its focus on bringing together people from diverse disciplines and backgrounds. It's a place where different voices are heard, and where collaboration leads to creative solutions. Professor Mamokgethi Phakeng, Vice-Chancellor of UCT, emphasizes the importance of inclusivity in driving innovation: "Innovation is about bringing people together—people with different perspectives, different experiences, different ways of thinking. At UCT, we believe that the best ideas come from collaboration, from creating a space where everyone's voice is valued."

UCT's Innovation Hub shows us that diversity and collaboration are key ingredients in the recipe for innovation. Educational leaders who prioritize these values can create environments where creativity and innovation thrive.

Embracing Continuous Improvement

Innovation isn't a one-time achievement; it's a continuous journey. Educational institutions must constantly seek out new knowledge, new skills, and new approaches. This requires a commitment to continuous improvement—a willingness to adapt, evolve, and learn.

The University of Helsinki in Finland embodies the spirit of continuous improvement. The university regularly reviews its programs and processes, seeking feedback from students and faculty to identify areas for enhancement. This commitment to ongoing learning has led to the development of new programs, the adoption of innovative teaching methods, and the integration of cutting-edge research into the curriculum. Professor Sari Lindblom, Rector of the University of Helsinki, speaks to this mindset:

"Innovation is not a destination; it's a journey. At the University of Helsinki, we're committed to constantly improving our programs and processes to provide the best possible education for our students. This means being open to change, being willing to learn, and always striving for excellence."

The University of Helsinki's approach teaches us that innovation is about more than just coming up with new ideas—it's about a commitment to continuous improvement. Educational leaders who embrace this mindset can ensure that their institutions remain at the forefront of educational excellence.

Building a culture of innovation in educational institutions is a journey that requires vision, courage, and a deep commitment to fostering an environment where creativity and experimentation are not only encouraged but celebrated. Innovation can take many forms, from adopting new technologies to fostering collaboration and inclusivity.

For educational leaders, the challenge is to create spaces where innovation can thrive—where faculty, staff, and students feel empowered to take risks, to experiment, and to explore new ideas. It's about integrating technology thoughtfully, fostering a collaborative environment, and committing to continuous improvement. By doing so, leaders can ensure that their institutions not only keep pace with the changing world but also play a leading role in shaping the future of education.

Key Takeaways

- Innovation in education goes beyond adopting the latest tools; it's about cultivating a mindset that values creativity, challenges the status quo, and seeks continuous improvement. Institutions like Amity University remind us that the heart of innovation lies in rethinking how we approach education.
- For innovation to thrive, educational leaders must create environments where experimentation and risk-taking are encouraged. Stanford University's culture of embracing failure as a learning tool shows the importance of allowing students and faculty to explore new ideas without fear.
- The thoughtful integration of technology is key to fostering innovation. Nanyang Technological University's approach highlights how technology can be a powerful enabler of learning when it aligns with an institution's educational goals.
- Diverse perspectives and collaborative efforts are essential for generating creative solutions. The University of Cape Town's Innovation Hub illustrates how bringing together people from different backgrounds can lead to more innovative and inclusive outcomes.
- Innovation is an ongoing journey that requires a commitment to learning and evolving. The University of Helsinki's focus on continuous improvement shows that institutions must constantly seek new ways to enhance their educational offerings to stay at the forefront of excellence.

CHAPTER XVI

The Role of Artificial Intelligence in Education

"The advance of technology is based on making it fit in so that you don't really even notice it, so it's part of everyday life. — Bill Gates"

Artificial Intelligence (AI) has made its way into nearly every aspect of our lives, and education is no exception. What once seemed like science fiction is now a reality, with AI transforming the way we teach, learn, and manage educational institutions. But as exciting as these developments are, they also raise important questions. How can AI truly enhance education without losing the human touch? What are the real benefits, and what are the potential pitfalls?

In this chapter, we're going to explore the powerful impact of AI in education. We'll look at real-life examples from around the world, showing how AI is already making a difference in classrooms, administration, and personalized learning. Along the way, we'll discuss the challenges and ethical considerations that come with integrating AI into education, always keeping in mind the need to balance innovation with the core values of teaching and learning.

A Personal Approach to Learning

Imagine walking into a classroom where every student is receiving the exact type of instruction they need, tailored to their strengths, weaknesses, and interests. It sounds idealistic, but this is what AI is beginning to make possible. By analyzing data on how students learn, AI can help educators design personalized learning experiences that adapt in real-time to each student's needs.

At Ashoka University, they're not just imagining this—they're doing it. In 2024, Ashoka introduced an AI-powered platform called "LearnX," designed to personalize learning paths for each student. The platform analyzes everything from how students interact with course materials to how they perform on assessments. It then provides tailored recommendations—whether it's suggesting additional resources, adjusting the pace of the course, or highlighting areas where the student might need extra help. Professor Malabika Sarkar, Vice-Chancellor of Ashoka University, shared her thoughts on the transformative power of AI in their classrooms: "We've always known that every student is unique, but AI has given us the tools to act on that knowledge in ways we couldn't before. With LearnX, we can offer a learning experience that's truly personalized, helping each student to reach their full potential."

Ashoka University shows how AI can bring a level of personalization to education that was previously unimaginable. It's about more than just efficiency—it's about meeting students where they are and helping them grow in the ways that matter most to them.

Making the Complex Simple

While AI is doing amazing things in the classroom, its impact on the administrative side of education is just as significant. Think about all the routine tasks that take up so much time—answering student queries, processing applications, managing schedules. AI has the potential to handle these tasks more efficiently, freeing up educators and administrators to focus on what they do best: supporting students.

The University of Edinburgh is a great example of how AI can revolutionize the administrative side of education. They've implemented an AI-driven chatbot named "EdAI" that takes care of a wide range of tasks, from answering student inquiries to handling course registrations and processing financial aid applications. EdAI doesn't just provide generic answers—it uses data from the university's systems to offer personalized, accurate responses, anytime, day or night. David Hume, Director of Student Services at the University of Edinburgh, explained how this technology is making a difference: "EdAI has transformed the way we support our students. By taking care of the routine tasks, it allows our staff to focus on more meaningful interactions with students. It's about making the complex simple, and ensuring that students get the help they need when they need it."

This shift shows how AI can be a powerful tool for improving efficiency in education, not by replacing human interaction, but by enhancing it. By automating the routine, AI allows educators and administrators to spend more time on the things that really matter.

Tailoring Education to Individual Needs

Personalized learning has long been the holy grail of education—every educator's dream is to meet each student exactly where they are. With AI, that dream is becoming more of a reality. By analyzing data on student performance, AI can help create learning experiences that are uniquely suited to each individual, making education more engaging and effective.

The University of New South Wales has taken personalized learning to the next level with their AI-driven platform, "SmartLearn." This platform uses machine learning algorithms to track students' progress in real-time, identifying where they might be struggling and offering targeted resources to help them improve. What's more, SmartLearn adapts to each student's preferred learning style, whether they thrive on visual content, interactive simulations, or text-based resources. Professor Ian Jacobs, President and Vice-Chancellor of UNSW, reflects on the impact of this approach: "SmartLearn is more than just a tool—it's a game-changer. By tailoring the learning experience to each student, we're not only improving academic outcomes but also making learning more enjoyable and meaningful. It's about giving students the support they need, when they need it, in the way that works best for them."

UNSW's SmartLearn platform is a perfect example of how AI can make education more personalized and student-centered, turning the traditional one-size-fits-all model on its head.

Navigating the Challenges of AI

Of course, with great power comes great responsibility. As we integrate AI into education, we must also be mindful of the ethical implications. Issues like data privacy, algorithmic bias, and the potential for AI to diminish the human elements of education are real concerns that need careful consideration.

At IIT Bombay, they're tackling these challenges head-on with their Ethics in AI Lab. This lab is dedicated to researching the ethical issues that arise with the use of AI in education and developing guidelines to ensure its responsible use. For example, they're working on algorithms that can detect and correct biases in AI-driven decision-making processes, ensuring that all students are treated fairly and equitably. Professor Subhasis Chaudhuri, Director of IIT Bombay, emphasizes the importance of this work: "AI has incredible potential to improve education, but we have to use it wisely. That means being vigilant about issues like bias and privacy, and making sure that our AI systems are transparent and accountable. We owe it to our students to get this right."

IIT Bombay's focus on ethics reminds us that as we embrace AI in education, we must also be mindful of the broader implications. It's not just about what AI can do, but about how we can use it to make education more fair and equitable.

Enhancing, Not Replacing

One of the most important things to remember about AI in education is that it's a tool—a powerful one, but still just a tool. The best uses of AI are those that enhance the capabilities of teachers, giving them new insights and resources to better support their students, without replacing the human connections that are at the heart of teaching.

McMaster University in Canada has embraced this philosophy with their "TeachAI" platform. This tool uses AI to analyze data from classroom interactions, assessments, and student feedback, providing teachers with actionable insights on how to improve their teaching methods. For example, TeachAI might suggest ways to differentiate instruction for students with different learning needs or offer real-time feedback during lessons. Dr. David Farrar, President and Vice-Chancellor of McMaster University, describes how AI is being used to support teachers: "TeachAI is like having an extra pair of eyes in the classroom. It gives our teachers the data-driven insights they need to tailor their instruction to the needs of their students, but it doesn't take over the teaching process. It's about empowering teachers to do what they do best, with a little help from AI."

McMaster's use of TeachAI shows how AI can be a valuable partner for teachers, helping them to be more effective in their roles without losing the personal connections that make education so impactful.

A Balanced Approach

As AI continues to evolve, its role in education will only grow. But as we've seen, the key to success is balance. AI has the potential to revolutionize education in profound ways, but it must be integrated thoughtfully, with a focus on enhancing—not replacing—the human elements of teaching and learning. Looking to the future, educational leaders will need to navigate these opportunities and challenges with care, ensuring that AI serves as a complement to, rather than a substitute for, the personal interactions and connections that are at the heart of education.

Artificial Intelligence offers incredible possibilities for the future of education. From personalized learning to streamlined administration and enhanced teacher effectiveness, AI has the potential to transform how we educate.

"The real power of AI lies in how it's used."

The challenge for educational leaders is to embrace AI in ways that enhance the learning experience, while also being mindful of the ethical implications and the need to preserve the human touch. By finding the right balance, we can harness the power of AI to create a more personalized, efficient, and equitable education system for all.

Key Takeaways

- AI offers the ability to tailor education to each student's unique needs, as seen with platforms like Ashoka University's LearnX. This personalization helps students engage more deeply and achieve their full potential by receiving support that's customized just for them.
- AI can handle routine administrative tasks efficiently, as demonstrated by the University of Edinburgh's EdAI chatbot. By automating these processes, educators and administrators can focus more on what truly

matters—supporting and engaging with students.

- The integration of AI in education must be guided by strong ethical principles, as IIT Bombay's Ethics in AI Lab emphasizes. Addressing issues like bias and data privacy ensures that AI enhances education without compromising fairness or equity.

- AI's greatest potential lies in augmenting the work of teachers, not replacing them. McMaster University's TeachAI platform shows how AI can provide valuable insights and support, empowering teachers to be even more effective in their roles.

- As AI continues to develop, its role in education will expand, but success depends on thoughtful integration. The challenge is to leverage AI's strengths while maintaining the human connections that are central to the educational experience.

CHAPTER XVII

Student-Centered Leadership in the Digital Age

"Education is not the filling of a pail, but the lighting of a fire. — William Butler Yeats"

In today's rapidly evolving educational landscape, the concept of student-centered leadership has taken on new significance. With the advent of digital tools and technologies, educators and leaders now have unprecedented opportunities to place students at the very heart of their institutions. But what does it truly mean to be student-centered in the digital age? How can leaders use technology to enhance student engagement, support, and success, without losing the personal touch that's so crucial to education?

This chapter explores the essence of student-centered leadership in the digital age, examining how innovative approaches and digital tools are reshaping the way institutions engage with and support their students. We'll look at how leaders are using technology to create more inclusive, responsive, and effective learning environments. By doing so, we'll uncover the key strategies that can help educational leaders guide their institutions toward a future where students are not just participants in their education but active, empowered drivers of their own learning experiences.

The Shift to Student-Centered Leadership

The shift from traditional, top-down leadership models to student-centered approaches marks a profound change in the way educational institutions are managed. At the core of this shift is the recognition that students are not passive recipients of knowledge, but active participants in their learning journeys. Student-centered leadership prioritizes the needs, voices, and experiences of students, ensuring that every decision made at the institutional level reflects their best interests.

The University of Queensland (UQ) has long been a proponent of student-centered leadership. In recent years, UQ has implemented a comprehensive strategy that places students at the center of every aspect of the university's operations. This strategy includes the creation of student advisory councils that provide direct input into decision-making processes, as well as the use of digital platforms that enable real-time feedback from students on their learning experiences. Professor Deborah Terry, Vice-Chancellor and President of UQ, underscores the importance of this approach: "At UQ, we believe that students should have a voice in shaping their education. Our student-centered leadership model ensures that we're not just teaching students but also learning from them. By listening to our students and incorporating their feedback, we're able to create a more responsive and supportive learning environment."

UQ's approach highlights a key principle of student-centered leadership: the importance of actively involving students in the governance and decision-making processes of the institution. This not only empowers students but also helps to create a more dynamic and adaptable educational environment.

Enhancing Student Engagement Through Digital Tools

In the digital age, the tools available to enhance student engagement are more varied and powerful than ever before. From learning management systems to mobile apps and virtual reality, technology provides new ways to connect with students, engage them in their studies, and support their success. However, the challenge for educational leaders is to ensure that these tools are used in ways that genuinely enhance the student experience.

Amrita Vishwa Vidyapeetham, one of India's leading universities, has embraced digital tools to enhance student engagement in innovative ways. The university has developed an AI-driven mobile app called "Amrita Engage," which offers students personalized learning resources, real-time academic support, and a platform to connect with peers and faculty. The app also features a gamified learning system that encourages student participation through rewards and recognition. Dr. P. Venkat Rangan, Vice-Chancellor of Amrita Vishwa Vidyapeetham, speaks to the impact of these digital tools: "Our goal with Amrita Engage is to create a more interactive and engaging learning experience for our students. By using AI and gamification, we're able to make learning more personalized and fun, which in turn drives better academic outcomes. But beyond the technology, it's about creating a sense of community and belonging among our students."

Amrita's use of digital tools illustrates how technology can be leveraged to enhance student engagement in meaningful ways. By focusing on the needs and preferences of students, educational leaders can use these tools to create more engaging and supportive learning environments.

Supporting Student Success with Data-Driven Insights

One of the most powerful applications of digital tools in education is the ability to gather and analyze data on student performance and behavior. These data-driven insights can help educational leaders identify at-risk students, tailor support services to individual needs, and make informed decisions that improve student outcomes.

Arizona State University has pioneered the use of data analytics to support student success. ASU's "Student Success Collaborative" is an integrated platform that uses predictive analytics to monitor student progress, identify those who may be struggling, and recommend targeted interventions. The platform provides advisors and faculty with real-time data on each student's academic journey, enabling them to offer personalized support at the right time. Dr. Michael Crow, President of ASU, explains the significance of this approach: "At ASU, we're committed to using data to enhance the student experience. By understanding the challenges our students face, we can provide them with the resources and support they need to succeed. Data-driven insights allow us to be proactive rather than reactive, ensuring that no student falls through the cracks."

ASU's use of data analytics demonstrates how digital tools can be harnessed to support student success in a targeted and effective manner. By leveraging these insights, educational leaders can create a more responsive and supportive educational environment that meets the diverse needs of their students.

The Human Element

While digital tools offer many benefits, they cannot replace the importance of personal connections in education. Student-centered leadership in the digital age requires a careful balance between leveraging technology and maintaining the human elements that are so crucial to learning and development.

At the University of Cape Town, the emphasis on student-centered leadership is reflected in their commitment to maintaining personal connections even as they embrace digital tools. UCT's "Student Success Program" combines the use of an AI-driven platform with regular, in-person meetings between students and mentors. This hybrid approach ensures that while students benefit from the efficiency and accessibility of digital tools, they also receive the personal support and guidance that is essential for their growth. Professor Mamokgethi Phakeng, Vice-Chancellor of UCT, emphasizes the importance of this balance: "Technology can do amazing things, but it can't replace the human touch. Our approach at UCT is to use digital tools to enhance, not replace, the personal relationships that are at the heart of education. By combining technology with human connection, we're able to provide our students with the best of both worlds."

UCT's approach highlights the need for educational leaders to ensure that the use of digital tools complements, rather than detracts from, the personal interactions that are so vital to student success. By maintaining this balance, leaders can create a more holistic and effective educational experience for their students.

Fostering Inclusivity and Accessibility in the Digital Age

Another key aspect of student-centered leadership is ensuring that all students have equal access to educational opportunities, regardless of their background or circumstances. Digital tools can play a significant role in promoting inclusivity and accessibility, but only if they are implemented thoughtfully and equitably.

The Open University in the UK has been a leader in using digital tools to promote inclusivity and accessibility in education. The university's online platform offers a wide range of resources that are designed to be accessible to students with disabilities, as well as those from underserved communities. The platform includes features such as screen readers, captioned videos, and interactive content that can be customized to meet the needs of individual learners. Professor Tim Blackman, Vice-Chancellor of the Open University, speaks to the importance of accessibility: "Our mission at the Open University is to make education accessible to everyone, no matter their circumstances. By leveraging digital tools, we're able to reach students who might not otherwise have the opportunity to pursue higher education. But accessibility isn't just about technology—it's about ensuring that every student feels welcome and supported in their learning journey."

The Open University's commitment to inclusivity and accessibility underscores the importance of using digital tools to create a more equitable educational environment. By prioritizing these values, educational leaders can ensure that all students have the opportunity to succeed.

Student-centered leadership in the digital age is about more than just adopting the latest technologies—it's about using those tools in ways that genuinely enhance the student experience. From increasing engagement and supporting success to fostering inclusivity and maintaining personal connections, digital tools offer a wide range of opportunities to create more responsive, supportive, and effective educational environments. It's about listening to students, using data to inform decisions, and ensuring that technology serves to enhance, rather than replace, the human elements of education.

In the end, the goal of student-centered leadership is to empower students to take control of their own learning journeys, equipping them with the tools, support, and opportunities they need to succeed in a rapidly changing world. By embracing this approach, educational leaders can guide their institutions toward a future where students are not just participants in their education but active, engaged, and empowered drivers of their own success.

Key Takeaways

- Student-centered leadership is about recognizing students as active partners in their education. Institutions like the University of Queensland demonstrate the importance of giving students a voice in decision-making, which leads to more responsive and dynamic learning environments.
- Digital tools can greatly enhance student engagement when used thoughtfully. Amrita Vishwa Vidyapeetham's AI-driven app shows that technology can make learning

more personalized, interactive, and enjoyable, fostering a stronger sense of community and belonging among students.

- Data-driven insights are powerful tools for supporting student success. Arizona State University's use of predictive analytics highlights how understanding students' challenges and needs can lead to proactive and targeted support, helping every student reach their full potential.
- While digital tools offer many benefits, they cannot replace the value of human connection in education. The University of Cape Town's approach of combining technology with personal mentoring reminds us that effective education requires both high-tech solutions and high-touch relationships.
- Digital tools have the potential to make education more inclusive, but this requires intentional effort. The Open University's commitment to accessibility demonstrates how technology can break down barriers, ensuring that all students, regardless of their circumstances, feel welcomed and supported.

CHAPTER XVIII

Curriculum Design for the Future

"Education is not preparation for life; education is life itself. — John Dewey"

As we stand on the cusp of a new era in education, the question of how to design curricula that prepare students for the future has never been more pressing. The digital age, with its rapid technological advancements and shifting societal needs, demands that we rethink traditional approaches to education. No longer can we rely solely on rote memorization or rigid disciplinary boundaries. Instead, the curricula of the future must be dynamic, adaptable, and deeply interconnected with the skills that students will need to thrive in a world that is increasingly complex and interconnected.

In this chapter, we'll explore how curricula need to evolve to meet these demands. We'll look at how digital literacy, critical thinking, and interdisciplinary studies are becoming essential components of a well-rounded education. Through examples from around the world, we'll see how institutions are reimagining what and how they teach, ensuring that their students are not only prepared for the jobs of tomorrow but also equipped to navigate the broader challenges of the 21st century.

The Importance of Digital Literacy

In today's world, digital literacy is as fundamental as reading, writing, and arithmetic. As technology continues to permeate every aspect of our lives, the ability to understand, navigate, and critically engage with digital tools and platforms is no longer a luxury—it's a necessity. But digital literacy goes beyond just knowing how to use technology; it's about understanding the broader implications of digital technologies on society, culture, and the economy.

Singapore has long been a global leader in education, and its approach to digital literacy is no exception. In 2024, the Ministry of Education in Singapore launched a nationwide initiative to integrate digital literacy across all levels of schooling. This initiative, known as the Digital Ready program, focuses not only on teaching students how to use digital tools but also on helping them understand the ethical, social, and economic impacts of these technologies. Mr. Chan Chun Sing, Singapore's Minister for Education, emphasizes the importance of this holistic approach: "Digital literacy is not just about technical skills; it's about understanding the world we live in. Our students need to be able to navigate the digital landscape critically and responsibly, and that's what we aim to achieve with the Digital Ready program."

Singapore's approach highlights the need for curricula that go beyond basic digital skills, encouraging students to think critically about the role of technology in their lives and in society.

Fostering Critical Thinking

If digital literacy is about understanding the tools, critical thinking is about knowing how to use them effectively. In an age where information is abundant and easily accessible, the ability to analyze, evaluate, and synthesize information is more important than ever. Critical thinking equips students with the skills to question assumptions, identify biases, and make informed decisions—a crucial capability in a world where misinformation is rife.

Ashesi University in Ghana has made critical thinking a cornerstone of its curriculum. At Ashesi, students are not just taught what to think but how to think. Through a curriculum that emphasizes inquiry-based learning and problem-solving, students are encouraged to question everything—from the content of their courses to the structures of society itself. Dr. Patrick Awuah, Founder and President of Ashesi University, believes that critical thinking is essential for developing ethical and effective leaders: "In today's world, where change is constant and challenges are complex, our students need to be able to think critically and act with integrity. At Ashesi, we aim to cultivate these skills, not just in the classroom, but throughout our students' lives."

Ashesi's commitment to critical thinking underscores the importance of curricula that challenge students to think deeply and critically about the world around them. This approach not only prepares students for the workforce but also for their roles as informed and engaged citizens.

The Rise of Interdisciplinary Studies

The challenges of the 21st century—climate change, global health crises, social inequality—are complex and interconnected. Addressing these challenges requires solutions that draw on knowledge from multiple disciplines. As such, there is a growing recognition of the need for interdisciplinary studies that break down the silos between subjects and encourage students to think across traditional boundaries.

O.P. Jindal Global University (JGU) is at the forefront of promoting interdisciplinary education. JGU offers a range of programs that combine disciplines such as law, business, international relations, and environmental studies, providing students with a holistic understanding of the complex issues facing the world today. The university's approach is based on the belief that the best solutions emerge when diverse perspectives come together. Professor C. Raj Kumar, Founding Vice-Chancellor of JGU, explains the importance of this approach: "The challenges we face today are not confined to any one discipline. Whether it's addressing climate change or fostering social justice, we need to draw on knowledge from multiple fields. At JGU, we encourage our students to think broadly and collaborate across disciplines to develop innovative solutions."

JGU's interdisciplinary programs demonstrate how curricula can be designed to reflect the interconnected nature of the world, preparing students to tackle the complex challenges of the future.

Integrating Soft Skills and Emotional Intelligence

In addition to digital literacy, critical thinking, and interdisciplinary knowledge, the future of education must also prioritize the development of soft skills and emotional intelligence. As automation and artificial intelligence take on more routine tasks, the skills that are uniquely human—such as empathy, communication, and teamwork—will become increasingly valuable.

Aalto University in Finland has integrated soft skills and emotional intelligence into its curriculum through innovative teaching methods that focus on collaboration and experiential learning. For example, the university's Design Factory is a multidisciplinary space where students work on real-world projects, often in partnership with industry. These projects require students to collaborate across disciplines, communicate effectively, and manage complex team dynamics—skills that are crucial in today's workforce. Professor Tuula Teeri, President of Aalto University, highlights the value of these skills: "In a rapidly changing world, technical knowledge alone is not enough. Our students need to be able to work effectively with others, navigate ambiguity, and lead with empathy. At Aalto, we believe that these skills are just as important as academic knowledge."

Aalto University's approach shows how curricula can be designed to develop the soft skills and emotional intelligence that are essential for success in the digital age.

Preparing for Lifelong Learning

Finally, as the pace of change accelerates, the ability to learn and adapt throughout one's life is becoming increasingly important. The future of work will require individuals to continuously update their skills and knowledge, and curricula must be designed to foster a mindset of lifelong learning.

Tsinghua University in China has embraced the concept of lifelong learning through its "Tsinghua Lifelong Learning Program." This initiative offers alumni and working professionals the opportunity to return to the university to update their skills and knowledge, reflecting the university's commitment to continuous education. The program includes online courses, executive education, and workshops that cover a wide range of topics, from digital transformation to leadership development. Professor Qiu Yong, President of Tsinghua University, emphasizes the importance of lifelong learning: "In a world that is constantly changing, learning cannot end with graduation. At Tsinghua, we are committed to supporting our students throughout their lives, helping them to stay relevant and thrive in their careers."

Tsinghua University's focus on lifelong learning demonstrates how curricula can be designed to support continuous education, ensuring that students are prepared not just for their first job, but for the many roles they will take on throughout their careers.

As we look to the future, it's clear that curricula must evolve to meet the demands of the digital age. This evolution requires a shift away from traditional, siloed approaches to education and toward a more holistic, integrated model that prepares students for the complex and interconnected world they will inherit. By integrating digital literacy, critical thinking, interdisciplinary studies, soft skills, and lifelong learning into their curricula, these institutions are setting a new standard for education in the 21st century.

As educators and leaders, our task is to continue this work, designing curricula that are not only relevant to the present but also adaptable to the future. By doing so, we can ensure that our students are equipped not just to survive but to thrive in a world that is constantly changing. The future of education lies in our ability to innovate, to think creatively, and to embrace the possibilities of the digital age while staying grounded in the timeless values of learning, collaboration, and human connection.

Key Takeaways

- In the digital age, understanding technology is just the beginning. True digital literacy involves critical engagement with digital tools and an understanding of their broader societal impacts, as seen in Singapore's comprehensive approach to integrating digital literacy into education.
- With the abundance of information available today, the ability to think critically, question assumptions, and make informed decisions is more important than ever. Ashesi University's focus on inquiry-based learning demonstrates the power of fostering critical thinking in students.
- The challenges of the 21st century are interconnected, requiring solutions that draw on multiple disciplines. O.P. Jindal Global University's interdisciplinary

programs show how breaking down academic silos can prepare students to tackle real-world issues more effectively.

- As automation increases, uniquely human skills like empathy, teamwork, and communication become even more valuable. Aalto University's emphasis on developing these skills highlights their importance in preparing students for the future workforce.
- In a rapidly changing world, education doesn't end with graduation. Institutions like Tsinghua University are leading the way in fostering a mindset of lifelong learning, ensuring that students remain adaptable and relevant throughout their careers.

CHAPTER XIX

Ethics and Digital Responsibility

"Ethics is knowing the difference between what you have a right to do and what is right to do. — Potter Stewart"

The digital age has brought about profound changes in education, offering new opportunities for learning, collaboration, and innovation. However, with these opportunities come significant ethical challenges that educational leaders must navigate carefully. As technology becomes more integrated into our educational systems, questions around digital responsibility, online behavior, and the broader impact of these technologies on society have come to the forefront. How do we ensure that the digital tools we use are ethical? How do we teach students to be responsible digital citizens? And what responsibilities do educational leaders have in guiding this transformation?

This chapter delves into the ethical challenges posed by digital transformation in education, exploring issues of digital citizenship, online behavior, and the responsibilities of educational leaders. We will examine how institutions are grappling with these complex issues, and how they are striving to create ethical frameworks that can guide the use of technology in education.

The Importance of Digital Citizenship

Digital citizenship refers to the responsible use of technology by anyone who uses computers, the internet, and digital devices to engage with society. In the context of education, it involves teaching students how to navigate the digital world safely, ethically, and responsibly. This includes understanding the rights and responsibilities of digital participation, protecting personal information, and being aware of the consequences of online actions.

Finland has long been a leader in education, and its approach to digital citizenship is no exception. In 2024, Finland's National Agency for Education updated its curriculum to include a comprehensive digital citizenship education program. This program teaches students not only the technical skills needed to use digital tools but also the ethical considerations involved in online behavior. Students learn about issues such as privacy, cyberbullying, and digital footprint management from an early age. Mr. Olli-Pekka Heinonen, Director-General of Finland's National Agency for Education, explains the rationale behind this initiative: "In a world where digital interactions are increasingly common, teaching our students to be responsible digital citizens is essential. It's not just about using technology—it's about using it wisely and ethically."

Finland's focus on digital citizenship highlights the need for educational systems to go beyond teaching technical skills and to emphasize the ethical dimensions of digital engagement.

Navigating Online Behaviour

With the rise of social media and other online platforms, students today face unique challenges in managing their online behavior. Educational institutions play a crucial role in guiding students to understand the implications of their actions in the digital space, fostering an environment where respectful and responsible online behavior is the norm.

At the University of Cape Town (UCT), a robust digital ethics program has been integrated into the curriculum, addressing the complexities of online behavior. The program, introduced in 2023, encourages students to critically examine their digital interactions, from social media posts to academic collaborations. It also includes workshops on digital etiquette, online harassment, and the long-term impact of a digital footprint. Professor Mamokgethi Phakeng, Vice-Chancellor of UCT, emphasizes the importance of this approach: "In the digital age, our actions online can have real-world consequences. At UCT, we are committed to educating our students not only in their academic pursuits but also in how they present themselves and interact with others in the digital world. This is a vital part of preparing them to be responsible, ethical leaders in their communities."

UCT's program serves as a model for how educational institutions can take an active role in shaping the online behavior of their students, ensuring that they understand the ethical implications of their digital actions.

The Responsibility of Educational Leaders

Educational leaders are at the forefront of navigating the ethical challenges posed by digital transformation. Their role involves not only implementing technology but also ensuring that its use aligns with the core values of education—equity, fairness, and respect for all participants. This includes making decisions about data privacy, digital equity, and the ethical use of AI and other technologies in the classroom.

IIT Delhi has been proactive in addressing the ethical responsibilities associated with digital transformation. In 2024, the institute launched an Ethics in Digital Education initiative, aimed at establishing guidelines for the ethical use of technology in teaching and research. This initiative includes a focus on data privacy, ensuring that student data is handled with the utmost care and respect. The institute has also introduced policies to address the ethical use of AI in educational settings, ensuring that these tools are used to enhance learning without compromising ethical standards. Professor V. Ramgopal Rao, Director of IIT Delhi, reflects on the importance of leadership in this area: "As educational leaders, we have a responsibility to ensure that the technologies we adopt in our institutions are used in ways that uphold our values. This means not only protecting the privacy and rights of our students but also ensuring that the tools we use promote fairness and inclusivity."

IIT Delhi's approach underscores the critical role that educational leaders play in guiding the ethical use of technology in education. Their decisions can have far-reaching implications for the integrity and effectiveness of educational practices.

Addressing Digital Equity

Digital equity is another critical issue that has come to the forefront with the increased reliance on technology in education. Digital equity ensures that all students, regardless of their socio-economic background, have access to the digital tools and resources they need to succeed. This includes access to reliable internet, digital devices, and the necessary skills to use these tools effectively.

In Kenya, the government has launched the Digital Literacy Program (DLP) to address the digital divide and promote digital equity among students. Since its inception, the program has provided millions of students in rural and underserved areas with access to digital devices and educational content. The DLP also includes teacher training programs to ensure that educators are equipped to integrate digital tools into their classrooms effectively. Dr. Julius Jwan, Principal Secretary of Kenya's State Department for Early Learning and Basic Education, highlights the importance of this initiative: "Digital equity is essential if we are to provide all our students with the opportunities they need to succeed. The Digital Literacy Program is a critical step in ensuring that no child is left behind in the digital age."

Kenya's DLP illustrates the importance of addressing digital equity as a fundamental component of ethical digital transformation in education. By ensuring that all students have access to digital tools and resources, educational institutions can help bridge the digital divide and promote inclusivity.

The Ethical Use of AI in Education

As AI becomes increasingly integrated into educational practices, the ethical implications of its use have become a significant concern. AI has the potential to transform education by providing personalized learning experiences and automating administrative tasks. However, it also raises questions about privacy, bias, and the potential for AI to replace human judgment in critical educational decisions.

The University of Edinburgh has taken a proactive approach to the ethical use of AI in education. In 2024, the university established the AI Ethics in Education Task Force, which is responsible for developing guidelines and policies to govern the use of AI in teaching and administration. The task force has focused on issues such as algorithmic bias, transparency, and the potential for AI to perpetuate existing inequalities in education. Professor Peter Mathieson, Principal and Vice-Chancellor of the University of Edinburgh, explains the university's approach: "AI has incredible potential to enhance education, but it must be used responsibly. At Edinburgh, we are committed to ensuring that our use of AI is transparent, fair, and aligned with our values. We believe that ethical considerations must be at the forefront of any decision to implement AI in our educational practices."

The University of Edinburgh's efforts highlight the importance of developing ethical frameworks for the use of AI in education. By addressing these issues proactively, educational institutions can harness the benefits of AI while minimizing the risks.

As education continues to evolve in response to digital transformation, the ethical challenges associated with this shift must be carefully considered. Issues such as digital citizenship, online behavior, digital equity, and the ethical use of AI are critical to ensuring that the benefits of digital transformation are realized without compromising the core values of education. By developing comprehensive ethical frameworks and taking proactive measures to promote digital responsibility, these institutions are setting a standard for the responsible use of technology in education.

Educational leaders play a pivotal role in guiding this transformation. Their decisions will shape the future of education, ensuring that it remains inclusive, equitable, and aligned with the ethical principles that underpin our society. As we move forward, it is essential that we continue to prioritize ethical considerations in all aspects of digital transformation, ensuring that technology serves to enhance, rather than undermine, the values that are central to education.

Key Takeaways

- Teaching students to be responsible digital citizens is as crucial as traditional education. It's about understanding the ethical implications of online behavior and using technology with integrity and respect, as demonstrated by Finland's comprehensive approach.
- Institutions play a vital role in shaping students' online interactions. By fostering a culture of respect and responsibility in the digital space, as seen at the University of Cape Town, educators can help students navigate the complexities of their online lives.
- Educational leaders bear the responsibility of ensuring that technology is used ethically within their institutions. IIT Delhi's initiative underscores the

importance of leadership in setting ethical guidelines that prioritize fairness, equity, and respect.

- Ensuring that all students have access to the digital tools and resources they need is a matter of equity and inclusion. Kenya's Digital Literacy Program exemplifies the importance of bridging the digital divide to provide equal opportunities for all students.
- While AI has the potential to transform education, it must be implemented with careful consideration of ethical issues such as bias and privacy. The University of Edinburgh's proactive approach highlights the need for transparency and fairness in the use of AI.

CHAPTER XX

The Role of EdTech Companies in Shaping the Future of Education

"The only thing worse than being blind is having sight but no vision. — Helen Keller"

As the digital revolution continues to transform nearly every aspect of our lives, the education sector is no exception. At the heart of this transformation are educational technology (EdTech) companies, which have emerged as powerful players in shaping how we teach, learn, and engage with knowledge. From developing innovative learning platforms to forging partnerships with educational institutions, these companies are not just providing tools—they're redefining the very landscape of education. But as we embrace these technological advancements, it's essential to examine the broader implications of EdTech's growing influence. How are these companies driving change in the education sector? What role do they play in shaping the future of education? And what are the implications for educational leaders who must navigate this rapidly evolving terrain?

In this chapter, we'll explore the impact of EdTech companies on education, looking at their innovations, partnerships, and the challenges they present to traditional educational models. We'll also see how these companies are influencing the direction of education, and what this means for the future of learning.

The Power of Innovation

At the core of the EdTech revolution is innovation. EdTech companies are not just digitizing existing educational practices—they're reimagining them. By leveraging the latest in technology, these companies are creating new ways of learning that are more interactive, personalized, and accessible.

upGrad, founded in 2015, has emerged as a leading EdTech company in India, specializing in higher education and professional development. The platform offers a wide array of online courses, including MBA programs, data science courses, and technology certifications, in collaboration with top universities like IIT Madras, Deakin University, and Liverpool John Moores University. upGrad's focus is on helping working professionals upskill and advance in their careers through flexible, high-quality online education. Ronnie Screwvala, the co-founder of upGrad, often highlights the company's mission: "Our aim is to make education accessible and relevant for professionals across the globe. By leveraging technology, we're able to offer world-class education that fits into the busy lives of working individuals, empowering them to achieve their career goals."

upGrad's success illustrates how EdTech companies are not just supplementing traditional education—they're creating opportunities for lifelong learning and career advancement, making education more accessible and aligned with the evolving needs of the global workforce.

Forging Partnerships

Another significant way EdTech companies are shaping the future of education is through partnerships with educational institutions. These collaborations are helping schools and universities to integrate technology into their curricula, expand their reach, and enhance the quality of education they provide.

Coursera, a leading global online learning platform, has forged partnerships with over 200 universities and organizations around the world, including institutions like the University of London, Yale University, and the Indian School of Business. These partnerships allow universities to offer their courses online, reaching millions of learners globally who might not otherwise have access to such high-quality education. Jeff Maggioncalda, CEO of Coursera, has often highlighted the transformative potential of these partnerships: "By collaborating with universities, we're able to bring world-class education to learners everywhere, regardless of their location or financial circumstances. This democratization of education is one of the most powerful impacts of EdTech."

Coursera's partnerships exemplify how EdTech companies can work hand-in-hand with educational institutions to expand access to education, enhance learning experiences, and reach a global audience.

The Challenge of Equity

While EdTech has the potential to democratize education, it also raises concerns about equity. The digital divide—where access to technology is unevenly distributed—remains a significant barrier in many parts of the world. EdTech companies, therefore, face the challenge of ensuring that their innovations do not exacerbate existing inequalities in education.

Khan Academy, a non-profit EdTech organization, has been at the forefront of addressing educational inequity through technology. The platform offers free, world-class education to anyone with access to the internet, with resources available in multiple languages and tailored to a wide range of learning levels. Sal Khan, the founder of Khan Academy, has consistently emphasized the importance of accessibility: "Our mission is to provide a free, world-class education to anyone, anywhere. We believe that every student deserves the opportunity to learn, regardless of where they come from or what resources they have."

Khan Academy's commitment to accessibility highlights the critical role that EdTech companies can play in bridging the digital divide, ensuring that technology-driven education is inclusive and equitable.

Navigating a Changing Landscape

As EdTech companies continue to grow in influence, educational leaders face new challenges and opportunities. The integration of technology into education is not just about adopting new tools—it's about rethinking the entire approach to teaching and learning. Educational leaders must be proactive in understanding the potential of these technologies while also considering their ethical implications and long-term impact on students.

Minerva Schools at KGI, a global university program headquartered in San Francisco, offers a case study in how educational leadership can adapt to the changing landscape of education. Minerva's curriculum is entirely designed around active learning and critical thinking, with all classes conducted online using a proprietary platform that encourages real-time interaction and collaboration. Ben Nelson, founder of Minerva, reflects on the role of leadership in this new educational model: "Educational leaders need to be visionaries who understand both the possibilities and the challenges of technology in education. At Minerva, we've built a model that leverages technology to create a more engaging and effective learning experience, but it requires a different kind of leadership—one that is agile, innovative, and deeply committed to student outcomes."

Minerva's approach demonstrates that as EdTech reshapes education, leaders must evolve to manage these changes effectively, ensuring that technology serves to enhance, rather than undermine, the educational experience.

What Lies Ahead?

Looking ahead, the influence of EdTech companies is likely to continue growing, with new innovations and partnerships shaping the future of education in ways we can only begin to imagine. However, this growth also brings with it significant responsibilities. EdTech companies must prioritize ethical considerations, ensuring that their products are used in ways that support rather than detract from the core mission of education.

Unacademy, another major player in the Indian EdTech scene, has made significant strides in leveraging technology to make high-quality education accessible to students across the country. With a focus on competitive exam preparation, Unacademy offers live classes, interactive sessions, and personalized learning paths. The platform has also begun exploring the use of AI to further personalize the learning experience, adapting content to meet the specific needs of each student. Gaurav Munjal, CEO of Unacademy, speaks to the future of EdTech: "We're only scratching the surface of what's possible with technology in education. The key is to keep the focus on the students—on improving their learning outcomes and ensuring that they have the tools they need to succeed. That's what will drive the future of EdTech."

Unacademy's forward-looking approach underscores the importance of keeping educational goals at the forefront of technological innovation, ensuring that as the industry evolves, it continues to serve the best interests of students.

The role of EdTech companies in shaping the future of education is undeniable. From driving innovation and forging partnerships to addressing issues of equity and influencing educational leadership, these companies are at the heart of a transformation that is redefining how we think about teaching and learning. However, with this influence comes great responsibility. As EdTech continues to evolve, it is essential that these companies remain committed to their core mission—enhancing education in ways that are ethical, inclusive, and focused on the needs of students.

Whether through innovation, partnerships, or a commitment to accessibility, these companies are setting the stage for the future of education. As we move forward, the challenge will be to ensure that this future is one where technology serves as a tool for empowerment, rather than an end in itself—a future where every student has the opportunity to learn, grow, and thrive in a rapidly changing world.

Key Takeaways

- EdTech companies like upGrad are not just digitizing existing educational models—they're transforming how we learn by making education more personalized, interactive, and accessible. This shift is creating new opportunities for lifelong learning and career advancement.

- Collaborations between EdTech platforms and educational institutions, as seen with Coursera's global partnerships, are democratizing education by providing access to world-class courses for learners around the globe, regardless of their location or financial background.

- While EdTech has the potential to democratize education, it also highlights the need to address the digital divide. Initiatives like Khan Academy's commitment to providing free, high-quality education ensure that all students, regardless of their resources, have the opportunity to learn and succeed.

- As EdTech reshapes the educational landscape, leaders must adapt by embracing technology while staying committed to ethical practices and student-centered outcomes. The example of Minerva Schools illustrates the need for visionary leadership that is agile, innovative, and deeply focused on enhancing student experiences.

- As EdTech companies continue to innovate, it's essential that they prioritize ethical considerations, ensuring that technology is used to support education's core mission—enhancing learning, promoting equity, and preparing students for a rapidly changing world.

CHAPTER XXI

Leading Educational Change

"Change is inevitable. Growth is optional. — John C. Maxwell"

Educational change is a complex, dynamic process that requires visionary leadership, strategic planning, and the ability to inspire others to embrace new ways of thinking and learning. Around the world, we see numerous examples of how effective leadership has been the driving force behind transformative educational initiatives. These initiatives not only improve the quality of education but also address pressing challenges such as inequality, access, and the need for skills that align with the demands of the 21st century.

In this chapter, we will explore several case studies from different countries, each highlighting the critical role of leadership in driving successful educational change. These examples will demonstrate how leaders in education can create lasting impact by fostering innovation, building strong partnerships, and prioritizing the needs of their students and communities.

Reimagining Early Childhood Education

Finland has long been recognized as a global leader in education, and in recent years, the country has undertaken a significant overhaul of its early childhood education system. This change was driven by the recognition that the first years of a child's life are crucial for their development and future success. The Finnish government, with strong leadership from the Ministry of Education and Culture, launched a nationwide initiative to enhance the quality and accessibility of early childhood education.

The initiative focused on three key areas: increasing the professional development of early childhood educators, integrating play-based learning into the curriculum, and ensuring that every child has access to high-quality early education regardless of their socioeconomic background. Ms. Li Andersson, Finland's Minister of Education, emphasized the importance of leadership in this transformation: "We knew that to truly make a difference in the lives of our youngest citizens, we needed to rethink how we approached early childhood education. This meant not just changing policies but also inspiring educators, parents, and communities to see the value in these early years."

The results have been remarkable. Finland now boasts some of the highest rates of participation in early childhood education in the world, and studies show that children who attend these programs perform better academically and socially as they progress through school. This case illustrates how strong leadership, coupled with a clear vision for change, can lead to significant improvements in educational outcomes.

Integrating Technology in Education

South Korea is another country that has made significant strides in education through strong leadership and innovative thinking. Recognizing the importance of technology in preparing students for the future, the South

Korean government launched the SMART Education initiative in 2020. This initiative aimed to transform classrooms across the country by integrating digital tools and resources into every aspect of the learning process.

The Ministry of Education, led by then-Minister Yoo Eun-hae, played a pivotal role in driving this change. The initiative included the widespread distribution of digital devices to students, the development of interactive online learning platforms, and extensive training for teachers to help them effectively incorporate technology into their teaching. Minister Yoo Eun-hae reflected on the challenges and rewards of leading such a large-scale change: "Transforming an education system as extensive as South Korea's requires not only resources but also a shared commitment among all stakeholders. Our success has been built on collaboration between government, educators, and the tech industry, ensuring that our students are equipped with the skills they need to thrive in the digital age."

Today, South Korea is recognized as one of the most technologically advanced education systems in the world. The SMART Education initiative has not only improved student engagement and achievement but has also positioned South Korea as a global leader in educational technology.

Expanding Access to Education through Leadership and Innovation

Rwanda's education system has undergone a remarkable transformation in recent years, driven by a national commitment to expanding access to education and improving quality. Following the devastating impact of the 1994 genocide, Rwanda faced the daunting challenge of rebuilding its education system from the ground up. Today, Rwanda's education sector is a testament to the power of leadership and innovation in driving change.

One of the most significant initiatives has been the implementation of the Nine-Year Basic Education program, which was later expanded to Twelve-Year Basic Education. This initiative, championed by the Rwandan government under the leadership of President Paul Kagame, aimed to provide free and compulsory education for all children, with a particular focus on girls and children from disadvantaged backgrounds. Dr. Valentine Uwamariya, Rwanda's Minister of Education, has played a crucial role in the continued success of this initiative. She notes, "Our goal was to ensure that every child in Rwanda, regardless of their circumstances, has the opportunity to receive a quality education. This required not only expanding access but also improving the quality of education through better teacher training, curriculum development, and the integration of technology."

The results have been transformative. Rwanda has achieved near-universal primary school enrollment, and significant progress has been made in secondary education as well. The government's focus on leadership, innovation, and inclusivity has helped create an education system that is more resilient and better equipped to meet the needs of all Rwandans.

Indigenous Education and Cultural Revitalization

In Canada, one of the most pressing issues in education has been addressing the historical and ongoing challenges faced by Indigenous communities. In recent years, there has been a growing recognition of the need to revitalize Indigenous languages and cultures through education. This has led to a number of successful initiatives aimed at promoting Indigenous-led education, with strong leadership from both Indigenous and non-Indigenous leaders.

One such initiative is the First Nations University of Canada (FNUniv), which has become a model for Indigenous education and cultural preservation. FNUniv offers programs that are rooted in Indigenous knowledge and traditions, providing students with a unique educational experience that honors their cultural heritage while also preparing them for the challenges of the modern world. Dr. Jacqueline Ottmann, President of FNUniv, has been a driving force behind the university's success. She explains, "Leading educational change within Indigenous communities requires a deep understanding of the cultural, social, and historical context. At FNUniv, we are committed to creating an educational environment that respects and uplifts Indigenous knowledge systems, empowering our students to become leaders in their communities."

The impact of FNUniv extends beyond the classroom. The university has played a crucial role in the broader movement for Indigenous rights and reconciliation in Canada, helping to build bridges between Indigenous and non-Indigenous communities. This case study highlights the importance of leadership that is deeply connected to the communities it serves, and the power of education as a tool for cultural revitalization and social change.

Reforming Vocational Education to Meet Workforce Needs

In Brazil, the challenge of aligning education with the needs of the labor market has been a key focus of recent educational reforms. Recognizing the importance of vocational education in addressing high youth unemployment rates, the Brazilian government, with leadership from the Ministry of Education, launched a comprehensive reform of the country's vocational education system.

The reform, known as the New Pathways initiative, aimed to make vocational education more relevant, flexible, and aligned with the demands of Brazil's growing economy. This included updating curricula to include more practical, hands-on training, expanding partnerships with industry, and increasing access to vocational programs for students from low-income backgrounds. Milton Ribeiro, Brazil's former Minister of Education, played a pivotal role in championing this reform. He stated, "Vocational education is critical to our nation's future. By equipping young people with the skills they need to succeed in the workforce, we are not only improving their individual prospects but also strengthening our economy as a whole."

The New Pathways initiative has already begun to show positive results, with increased enrollment in vocational programs and higher employment rates among graduates. This case study underscores the importance of leadership that is responsive to the needs of the labor market and committed to creating educational opportunities that prepare students for meaningful careers.

These case studies illustrate the diverse ways in which leadership can drive successful educational change.

Whether it's reimagining early childhood education, integrating technology into classrooms, expanding access to education, revitalizing Indigenous cultures, or aligning vocational education with workforce needs, these initiatives highlight the critical role of leaders who are visionary, collaborative, and deeply committed to the well-being of their students and communities.

As we look to the future of education, it is clear that leadership will continue to be the key to navigating the complex challenges and opportunities that lie ahead. By learning from these examples, educational leaders around the world can draw inspiration and insights to guide their own efforts to create lasting, positive change in their schools, universities, and communities.

Key Takeaways

- The case studies demonstrate that transformative educational initiatives, whether in Finland's early childhood education or South Korea's technological integration, are driven by leaders with a clear, forward-thinking vision that aligns with the needs of their communities.
- Successful educational change is often the result of strong collaboration between governments, educators, and communities. Rwanda's focus on inclusive education and Canada's Indigenous-led educational initiatives show the power of collective effort in addressing systemic challenges.
- The success of educational reforms depends on understanding and respecting the cultural and social context in which they are implemented. Canada's efforts

in Indigenous education highlight the importance of cultural revitalization, while Brazil's vocational reforms reflect responsiveness to economic needs.

- Leaders who are responsive to evolving challenges—whether it's integrating technology in South Korea or aligning vocational training with the labor market in Brazil—demonstrate the importance of flexibility and adaptability in education.
- Across all case studies, the role of education as a means to empower individuals and communities is evident. Whether through improving workforce readiness in Brazil or fostering resilience in Rwanda, these initiatives show that education, when led effectively, can drive significant social and economic progress.

CHAPTER XXII

Future-Ready Skills and Competencies

"The illiterate of the 21ˢᵗ century will not be those who cannot read and write, but those who cannot learn, unlearn, and relearn. — Alvin Toffler"

As we look toward the future, the landscape of work is evolving at a pace that challenges traditional notions of education and professional development. The skills and competencies that students need to thrive in tomorrow's workforce are vastly different from those that were prioritized just a decade ago. The Fourth Industrial Revolution, driven by advancements in technology, artificial intelligence, and global interconnectedness, is reshaping industries and creating new demands on the workforce.

In this context, educational leaders face the critical task of preparing students for a world that is dynamic, uncertain, and increasingly reliant on complex, interdisciplinary knowledge. This chapter explores the essential skills and competencies that will define success in the future workforce and examines how educational institutions can adapt to ensure that students are not just equipped for the jobs of today, but are agile, innovative, and resilient enough to navigate the challenges and opportunities of tomorrow.

The Shifting Landscape of Work

The future of work is characterized by rapid technological advancements and shifts in the global economy that are disrupting traditional job roles and creating new opportunities. Automation, artificial intelligence, and machine learning are transforming industries, making some jobs obsolete while creating entirely new fields of work. For example, according to the World Economic Forum's Future of Jobs Report 2024, nearly half of all work activities could be automated by 2030, yet new jobs in technology, data analysis, and digital content creation are expected to grow exponentially.

In response to these changes, companies like Infosys have taken proactive steps to prepare their workforce for the future. Recognizing that many existing roles would be transformed by technology, Infosys launched a massive reskilling initiative aimed at training over 100,000 employees in digital skills, including artificial intelligence, data analytics, and cloud computing. This initiative not only helps employees remain relevant in their current roles but also equips them with the skills needed to transition into new areas of growth within the company. Salil Parekh, CEO of Infosys, highlights the importance of such efforts: "The future of work will be defined by the ability to adapt to new technologies and continuously learn new skills. Our reskilling programs are designed to ensure that our workforce is future-ready, capable of leading the next wave of innovation."

Infosys' approach underscores the importance of lifelong learning and adaptability—key competencies that educational institutions must instill in students to prepare them for the evolving job market.

Critical Thinking and Problem-Solving

As automation takes over routine tasks, the ability to think critically and solve complex problems will become increasingly valuable. Critical thinking involves analyzing information, questioning assumptions, and making decisions based on evidence and logic. Problem-solving, on the other hand, requires the ability to identify challenges, evaluate potential solutions, and implement strategies effectively.

The University of Tokyo has integrated critical thinking and problem-solving into its core curriculum as part of its initiative to prepare students for the demands of the modern workforce. Through interdisciplinary courses that combine science, technology, and humanities, students are encouraged to tackle real-world problems using a holistic approach. This initiative, known as "Global Science Campus," has been instrumental in fostering a culture of innovation and critical inquiry among students. Dr. Teruo Fujii, President of the University of Tokyo, explains the rationale behind this approach: "In a world that is increasingly complex, the ability to think critically and solve problems is not just a skill—it's a necessity. Our goal is to produce graduates who can navigate uncertainty, challenge conventional thinking, and develop solutions that have a meaningful impact on society."

By emphasizing critical thinking and problem-solving, the University of Tokyo is equipping students with the cognitive tools they need to succeed in a rapidly changing world.

Emotional Intelligence and Interpersonal Skills

While technical skills are essential, the future of work will also place a premium on emotional intelligence (EQ) and interpersonal skills. Emotional intelligence involves the ability to understand and manage one's own emotions, as well as empathize with others and navigate social complexities. As automation and AI take over more tasks, the uniquely human ability to connect, collaborate, and lead will become increasingly important.

Malaysia's HRDF has recognized the importance of emotional intelligence in the workplace and has incorporated EQ training into its workforce development programs. These programs focus on building leadership, communication, and team collaboration skills, ensuring that employees are not only technically proficient but also capable of thriving in dynamic, people-centered environments. Datuk Shahul Hameed Dawood, Chief Executive of HRDF, emphasizes the role of EQ in future success: "In a world where technology is constantly evolving, emotional intelligence will set individuals apart. The ability to connect with others, lead teams, and manage change is what will drive success in the future workplace."

HRDF's focus on emotional intelligence highlights the need for educational institutions to go beyond technical training and cultivate the interpersonal skills that will enable students to lead and collaborate effectively in diverse, global teams.

Digital Literacy and Technological Proficiency

In an increasingly digital world, proficiency with technology is no longer optional—it's essential. Digital literacy goes beyond basic computer skills to include the ability to navigate complex digital environments, understand the ethical implications of technology use, and leverage digital tools to solve problems and create new opportunities.

KAUST has taken a leading role in promoting digital literacy and technological proficiency through its Digital Learning Program. This initiative provides students with advanced training in areas such as data science, cybersecurity, and AI, while also emphasizing the ethical considerations of technology use. By integrating digital literacy across all disciplines, KAUST ensures that its graduates are equipped to thrive in a technology-driven world. Dr. Tony Chan, President of KAUST, underscores the importance of digital literacy: "In the digital age, the ability to understand and use technology is as fundamental as reading and writing. Our goal is to prepare students not only to use technology but to innovate with it, driving progress in their fields and contributing to the broader society."

KAUST's approach reflects the critical need for educational institutions to embed digital literacy into their curricula, ensuring that students are prepared to navigate and shape the future of the digital landscape.

Creativity and Innovation

As the world becomes more automated, creativity and innovation will become key differentiators in the workforce. Creativity involves the ability to generate new ideas, think outside the box, and approach problems from novel angles. Innovation, on the other hand, requires the ability to turn creative ideas into tangible solutions that add value to society.

Aalto University in Finland has become a hub for creativity and innovation, particularly through its interdisciplinary programs that bring together students from different fields to work on collaborative projects. One of the university's flagship initiatives, the Design Factory, serves as a space where students can experiment with new ideas, prototype solutions, and develop entrepreneurial ventures. This emphasis on creativity and hands-on learning has positioned Aalto as a leader in fostering the skills that will drive future innovation. Ilkka Niemelä, President of Aalto University, reflects on the importance of creativity: "In a rapidly changing world, creativity is the engine of progress. At Aalto, we believe that fostering a culture of innovation is essential to preparing students for the future. We encourage them to take risks, challenge assumptions, and push the boundaries of what is possible."

Aalto University's focus on creativity and innovation underscores the importance of cultivating these competencies in students, enabling them to be the innovators and problem-solvers of the future.

Lifelong Learning and Adaptability

In a world where the only constant is change, the ability to continuously learn and adapt is crucial. Lifelong learning involves the pursuit of knowledge and skills throughout one's life, allowing individuals to stay relevant in an ever-evolving job market. Adaptability, meanwhile, is the ability to adjust to new conditions, embrace change, and remain resilient in the face of uncertainty.

The National University of Singapore has made lifelong learning a cornerstone of its educational philosophy. Through its Lifelong Learning Initiative, NUS offers a wide range of continuing education programs, micro-credentials, and flexible learning options that allow students and alumni to update their skills throughout their careers. This initiative is designed to ensure that graduates remain competitive in a rapidly changing job market, with the agility to pivot to new opportunities as they arise. Professor Tan Eng Chye, President of NUS, articulates the importance of lifelong learning: "The future of work will be defined by continuous change. To thrive in this environment, individuals must embrace lifelong learning and be willing to adapt to new challenges and opportunities. At NUS, we are committed to supporting our students and alumni in their lifelong journey of learning and growth."

NUS's commitment to lifelong learning highlights the need for educational institutions to instill a mindset of continuous development in their students, preparing them to navigate the complexities of the future workforce.

Global Competence and Cross-Cultural Understanding

As the world becomes more interconnected, the ability to work effectively across cultures and navigate global contexts will be essential. Global competence involves understanding and appreciating cultural differences, communicating effectively with people from diverse backgrounds, and collaborating on international teams. Cross-cultural understanding, meanwhile, is the ability to recognize and respect cultural diversity, fostering inclusive environments that embrace different perspectives.

The United Nations University has been at the forefront of promoting global competence and cross-cultural understanding through its Global Leadership Program. This program brings together students from around the world to engage in collaborative research, policy analysis, and leadership training on issues such as sustainability, peace, and development. By fostering a global mindset, UNU prepares students to tackle the complex challenges of an interconnected world. David M. Malone, Rector of UNU, emphasizes the importance of global competence: "In today's interconnected world, the ability to understand and engage with different cultures is not just a skill—it's a necessity. Our Global Leadership Program is designed to equip students with the knowledge, skills, and perspectives they need to thrive in a diverse and rapidly changing global environment."

UNU's focus on global competence underscores the need for educational institutions to prepare students for the complexities of working in a globalized world, where cross-cultural collaboration and understanding are key to success.

Ethical Leadership and Social Responsibility

As the future workforce navigates an increasingly complex world, the need for ethical leadership and social responsibility becomes paramount. Ethical leadership involves making decisions that are guided by a strong moral compass, prioritizing the well-being of individuals and communities. Social responsibility, on the other hand, requires individuals and organizations to act in ways that contribute positively to society, addressing issues such as inequality, sustainability, and human rights.

Ashoka University has made ethical leadership and social responsibility central to its mission, particularly through its Young India Fellowship program. This program, which brings together young leaders from diverse backgrounds, emphasizes the importance of ethical decision-making, social impact, and community engagement. Through coursework, mentorship, and fieldwork, students are encouraged to reflect on their values and take action to address societal challenges. Dr. Pramath Raj Sinha, Founder and Chairman of Ashoka University, articulates the university's commitment to ethical leadership: "In a world that is increasingly complex and interconnected, ethical leadership is more important than ever. At Ashoka, we believe that education should not only equip students with knowledge and skills but also instill a sense of responsibility to use those skills for the greater good."

Ashoka University's focus on ethical leadership and social responsibility highlights the importance of preparing students to lead with integrity, making decisions that are not only effective but also just and compassionate.

As we look to the future, it is clear that the skills and competencies required to thrive in the workforce are evolving rapidly. Educational institutions have a critical role to play in ensuring that students are equipped with the knowledge, skills, and mindset needed to navigate this complex and dynamic landscape. From critical thinking and emotional intelligence to digital literacy and global competence, the competencies discussed in this chapter represent the foundation for success in the 21st century. Educational leaders around the world are rising to the challenge of preparing students for the future. By fostering a culture of innovation, lifelong learning, and ethical leadership, these institutions are ensuring that their graduates are not only ready for the jobs of tomorrow but are also equipped to drive positive change in their communities and beyond.

As educational leaders, the responsibility to prepare future-ready students is both a challenge and an opportunity. By embracing this responsibility with vision, creativity, and a commitment to excellence, we can ensure that our students are not just participants in the future workforce but leaders who will shape it for the better.

Key Takeaways

- In a rapidly changing world, the ability to continuously learn and adapt is essential. Institutions like the National University of Singapore emphasize lifelong learning to ensure that graduates remain competitive and agile in the face of evolving challenges.
- As routine tasks become automated, critical thinking and problem-solving skills are becoming fundamental.

The University of Tokyo's approach to integrating these skills into the curriculum highlights the necessity of preparing students to navigate complexity with logic and creativity.

- In an increasingly automated world, emotional intelligence and interpersonal skills are becoming critical differentiators. Malaysia's HRDF initiative shows that the ability to connect, lead, and collaborate effectively is crucial for future success.

- Proficiency in digital tools and the ability to innovate are essential for thriving in the digital age. Institutions like KAUST and Aalto University emphasize the importance of digital literacy and creativity in preparing students to be innovators in their fields.

- As the world becomes more interconnected, the ability to work across cultures and lead with integrity is increasingly important. Programs at the United Nations University and Ashoka University demonstrate the value of global competence and ethical leadership in preparing students to address global challenges responsibly.

CHAPTER XXIII

Governance and Policy in the Digital Age

"Policy is a wise guess, and the art of administration is to make that guess come true. — Felix Frankfurter"

The advent of the digital age has ushered in unprecedented changes across all sectors, and education is no exception. As technology continues to evolve at a breakneck pace, educational governance and policy must adapt to meet new challenges and seize emerging opportunities. The digital age presents both a catalyst for innovation and a disruptor to traditional educational practices, demanding a reimagining of how institutions are governed and how policies are crafted and implemented.

This chapter delves into the evolving landscape of educational governance and policy in the digital era. It explores the challenges faced by educational leaders in navigating this complex environment, from data privacy concerns to the equitable access to technology. At the same time, it highlights the opportunities for transforming education through innovative policy frameworks that embrace the potential of digital tools while safeguarding core educational values.

The Digital Transformation of Educational Governance

The digital age has fundamentally altered how educational institutions are governed. Traditional governance structures, which often relied on hierarchical decision-making and bureaucratic processes, are increasingly being challenged by the need for more agile, responsive, and transparent models of governance. Digital tools offer the potential to enhance decision-making processes, increase stakeholder engagement, and improve the overall effectiveness of governance.

Estonia, a small European nation, has emerged as a global leader in digital governance. The country's e-Governance model, which extends to its education system, provides a compelling example of how digital tools can revolutionize governance. Estonia's education system is integrated into a broader digital infrastructure that allows for real-time data sharing, streamlined administrative processes, and enhanced transparency. The e-School system, for instance, connects students, parents, teachers, and administrators in a single digital platform, enabling efficient communication and decision-making. This system allows parents to monitor their children's progress, teachers to manage their classrooms more effectively, and administrators to make data-driven decisions. The transparency and accessibility of this model have significantly improved the governance of Estonia's educational institutions. Kersti Kaljulaid, former President of Estonia, has often highlighted the importance of digital governance in education: "In the digital age, governance must be as agile and connected as the world it operates in. Our e-Governance model in education is designed to empower all stakeholders, making decision-making more transparent, data-driven, and inclusive."

Estonia's approach demonstrates how digital tools can be leveraged to create a more dynamic and effective governance framework, setting a precedent for other nations seeking to modernize their educational systems.

Challenges in Educational Governance

While digital tools offer significant benefits, they also present challenges that educational leaders must navigate. One of the most pressing challenges is the digital divide—the gap between those who have access to technology and those who do not. This divide can exacerbate existing inequalities in education, making it difficult for all students to benefit equally from digital learning opportunities.

India's National Education Policy (NEP) 2020 addresses the challenge of the digital divide head-on. The policy recognizes that access to digital resources is unevenly distributed across the country, particularly in rural and economically disadvantaged areas. To address this, the NEP includes provisions for increasing digital infrastructure in schools, promoting digital literacy, and ensuring that all students have access to quality digital content. Dr. K. Kasturirangan, the architect of the NEP 2020, emphasizes the importance of equity in digital education: "The digital age presents incredible opportunities for transforming education, but these opportunities must be accessible to all. Our policy aims to bridge the digital divide, ensuring that no student is left behind in the journey toward a more connected and technologically advanced education system."

India's approach to addressing the digital divide through policy highlights the importance of equity in digital governance. Educational leaders must ensure that digital tools are implemented in ways that promote inclusivity and equal access to learning opportunities.

Data Privacy and Security

As educational institutions increasingly rely on digital tools for administration and instruction, the issue of data privacy and security has become a critical concern. The collection, storage, and use of student data must be carefully managed to protect privacy and comply with legal and ethical standards. Educational leaders must navigate the complexities of data governance, balancing the benefits of data-driven decision-making with the need to safeguard sensitive information.

The European Union's General Data Protection Regulation (GDPR) has set a high standard for data privacy and security, including within the education sector. Educational institutions across Europe are required to comply with GDPR, which mandates strict guidelines for the handling of personal data. This includes obtaining consent from students or their guardians, ensuring data is stored securely, and providing individuals with the right to access and control their personal information. In response to GDPR, many European universities and schools have implemented robust data governance frameworks. These frameworks include data protection officers, regular audits, and comprehensive training programs for staff to ensure compliance with the regulation. Andrus Ansip, former Vice President of the European Commission for the Digital Single Market, underscores the importance of data privacy in education: "In the digital age, data is a powerful tool, but it must be used responsibly. GDPR provides a framework for protecting personal data, ensuring that students' privacy is respected while enabling educational institutions to leverage data for better decision-making."

The implementation of GDPR in the education sector highlights the need for educational leaders to prioritize data privacy and security, ensuring that the use of digital tools does not compromise the trust and safety of students.

Policy Innovation

While the digital age presents challenges, it also offers unprecedented opportunities for policy innovation. Educational leaders have the chance to craft policies that harness the power of digital tools to enhance learning, improve administrative efficiency, and foster greater collaboration among stakeholders. Forward-thinking policies can drive the adoption of new technologies, support professional development for educators, and create more flexible and personalized learning environments.

Singapore's Smart Nation initiative is a prime example of policy innovation in the digital age. The initiative, which aims to transform Singapore into a digitally empowered nation, includes a strong focus on education. The Ministry of Education has developed a series of policies under the Smart Nation framework that promote the integration of technology into teaching and learning. One key policy is the National Digital Literacy Programme (NDLP), which equips students with essential digital skills and promotes the use of digital tools in the classroom. The NDLP also provides professional development opportunities for teachers, ensuring that they are prepared to effectively use technology in their teaching. Additionally, the Ministry has implemented policies to support data-driven decision-making in schools, using analytics to track student progress and inform educational strategies. Lawrence Wong, Singapore's Deputy Prime Minister and Minister for Finance, who has played a key role in the Smart Nation initiative, reflects on the importance of policy innovation: "In the digital age, education policies must be forward-looking and adaptable. Our Smart Nation initiative is about more than just technology—it's about creating an environment where students and educators can thrive in a rapidly changing world."

Singapore's Smart Nation initiative illustrates how innovative policies can drive the digital transformation of education, positioning students and educators to succeed in the 21st century.

Ethical Considerations in Digital Governance

As educational institutions embrace digital tools, ethical considerations must be at the forefront of governance and policy decisions. The use of technology in education raises important questions about equity, access, and the potential for bias in data-driven decision-making. Educational leaders must ensure that digital governance frameworks are guided by ethical principles that prioritize the well-being of students and the broader community.

In 2024, UNESCO released its Ethical AI in Education Guidelines, a comprehensive framework designed to guide the responsible use of artificial intelligence in educational settings. These guidelines address the ethical challenges posed by AI, including issues of bias, transparency, and the impact of AI on human rights. The guidelines emphasize the importance of human oversight in AI decision-making processes and call for policies that ensure AI is used to enhance educational outcomes without compromising ethical standards. Stefania Giannini, Assistant Director-General for Education at UNESCO, has been a vocal advocate for ethical AI in education: "AI offers tremendous potential to transform education, but it must be used responsibly. Our guidelines provide a roadmap for educational leaders to navigate the ethical complexities of AI, ensuring that technology serves the best interests of students and society."

UNESCO's Ethical AI in Education Guidelines highlight the critical role of ethics in digital governance, reminding educational leaders that the adoption of new technologies must be carefully balanced with the need to protect the rights and dignity of all students.

Leadership in the Digital Age

The digital age demands a new kind of leadership—one that is agile, visionary, and capable of navigating change and uncertainty. Educational leaders must be prepared to lead their institutions through the complexities of digital transformation, fostering a culture of innovation while ensuring that core educational values are upheld. This requires a deep understanding of both the opportunities and challenges presented by digital tools, as well as the ability to build consensus among diverse stakeholders.

Harvard University has developed a Digital Leadership Framework designed to equip its leaders with the skills and knowledge needed to navigate the digital age. This framework includes a series of professional development programs focused on digital literacy, data-driven decision-making, and ethical governance. Leaders are trained to think critically about the impact of digital tools on education and to develop strategies that leverage technology to enhance learning while addressing potential risks. Larry Bacow, President of Harvard University, has emphasized the importance of digital leadership: "In the digital age, leadership is about more than just managing change—it's about shaping the future. Our Digital Leadership Framework is designed to empower our leaders to think creatively, act ethically, and drive innovation in ways that benefit our entire community."

Harvard's approach to digital leadership underscores the importance of equipping educational leaders with the tools they need to effectively govern in the digital age, ensuring that they are prepared to lead their institutions through the challenges and opportunities of the 21st century.

The digital age is transforming the landscape of educational governance and policy, presenting both challenges and opportunities for educational leaders. From the integration of digital tools in governance models to the ethical considerations of AI, the role of educational leaders is becoming increasingly complex and dynamic. As we move forward, it is clear that the digital age requires a reimagining of how education is governed and how policies are crafted and implemented. Educational leaders must be prepared to embrace innovation, prioritize equity, and uphold ethical standards, all while navigating the uncertainties of a rapidly changing world. By doing so, they can ensure that their institutions not only survive but thrive in the digital era, providing students with the education they need to succeed in the 21st century.

As educational leaders, the responsibility to lead with vision, creativity, and integrity has never been more important. By embracing this responsibility, we can create a future where education is more accessible, equitable, and effective than ever before.

Key Takeaways

- The digital age demands a shift from traditional hierarchical governance to more agile, transparent, and responsive models. Estonia's e-Governance model exemplifies how digital tools can enhance decision-making and stakeholder engagement, setting a benchmark for educational governance in the digital era.
- As technology becomes integral to education, addressing the digital divide is crucial to ensuring that all students have equal access to learning opportunities. India's National Education Policy 2020 highlights the importance of equity in digital governance, emphasizing the need for inclusive policies that leave no student behind.
- The increasing reliance on digital tools in education raises significant concerns about data privacy and security. The European Union's GDPR sets a high standard for protecting student data, reminding educational leaders that responsible data governance is critical to maintaining trust and compliance in the digital age.
- Forward-thinking policies are key to harnessing the opportunities presented by the digital age. Singapore's Smart Nation initiative demonstrates how innovative policies can lead to the successful integration of

technology in education, preparing students and educators for the challenges of the 21st century.

- As digital tools become more prevalent in education, ethical considerations must guide governance and policy decisions. UNESCO's Ethical AI in Education Guidelines emphasize the need for responsible use of technology, ensuring that educational leaders prioritize the well-being and rights of students in their digital transformation efforts.

CHAPTER XXIV

Sustainability and Education

"Sustainability is not just about doing less harm. It's about doing more good. — Jochen Zeitz"

In the face of global challenges such as climate change, resource depletion, and environmental degradation, the role of education in promoting sustainability has never been more critical. Educational institutions are uniquely positioned to lead the charge in fostering a sustainable future by integrating sustainable practices into their operations, curricula, and community engagement efforts. As centers of knowledge creation and dissemination, these institutions have the power to shape the values and behaviors of future generations, equipping them with the skills and mindsets necessary to address the pressing environmental issues of our time.

This chapter explores the intersection of sustainability and education, examining how educational institutions can lead in promoting sustainable practices and preparing students for a sustainable future. Through a combination of recent examples from India and around the world, the chapter will highlight innovative approaches to sustainability in education and discuss the challenges and opportunities that lie ahead.

The Role of Educational Institutions in Promoting Sustainability

Educational institutions are not just places of learning; they are microcosms of society where future leaders, policymakers, and citizens are shaped. By embedding sustainability into their core values and practices, these institutions can serve as role models for their communities and the broader world. This involves not only teaching about sustainability but also demonstrating it through campus operations, research initiatives, and community outreach.

The TERI (The Energy and Resources Institute) School of Advanced Studies in New Delhi is a leading example of how educational institutions can integrate sustainability into every aspect of their mission. TERI SAS offers specialized programs in sustainable development, climate change, and renewable energy, equipping students with the knowledge and skills needed to address global environmental challenges. The campus itself is a living laboratory for sustainability, featuring energy-efficient buildings, water conservation systems, and waste management practices that minimize its environmental footprint. Dr. Leena Srivastava, a former Vice-Chancellor of TERI SAS, emphasizes the importance of practice in education: "Sustainability cannot just be taught in classrooms; it must be lived. At TERI SAS, we strive to create an environment where sustainability is woven into the fabric of everyday life, so our students leave not just with knowledge, but with the experience of living sustainably."

TERI SAS's approach underscores the importance of leading by example. By creating a sustainable campus and offering programs that focus on real-world applications, the institution prepares students to be effective advocates and practitioners of sustainability in their future careers.

Integrating Sustainability into the Curriculum

To prepare students for a sustainable future, educational institutions must go beyond traditional environmental science courses and embed sustainability across the curriculum. This interdisciplinary approach ensures that all students, regardless of their field of study, gain an understanding of how their discipline intersects with environmental issues and what they can do to promote sustainability in their future careers.

The University of British Columbia has been a pioneer in integrating sustainability into its curriculum. UBC's Sustainability Initiative, launched in 2010, aims to embed sustainability into all aspects of the university's operations and academic offerings. The initiative includes a comprehensive curriculum integration project, which supports faculty in incorporating sustainability into their courses across disciplines—from engineering and business to arts and humanities. Professor John Robinson, who spearheaded the UBC Sustainability Initiative, reflects on the importance of this approach: "Sustainability is not just an environmental issue; it's a social, economic, and ethical one. By integrating sustainability into the curriculum, we ensure that every student, regardless of their major, graduates with the knowledge and skills needed to contribute to a sustainable future."

UBC's commitment to sustainability in education highlights the importance of interdisciplinary learning in addressing complex global challenges. By embedding sustainability across the curriculum, UBC ensures that its graduates are well-equipped to apply sustainable principles in diverse fields.

Research and Innovation for a Sustainable Future

Educational institutions are also at the forefront of research and innovation in sustainability. Through cutting-edge research, universities and colleges can develop new technologies, strategies, and policies that address environmental challenges and promote sustainable development. These research efforts not only contribute to global knowledge but also provide students with hands-on experience in tackling real-world problems.

Wageningen University & Research (WUR) in the Netherlands is a world leader in agricultural and environmental research, with a strong focus on sustainability. WUR's research initiatives cover a wide range of topics, including sustainable agriculture, food security, and climate change mitigation. The university's commitment to sustainability is reflected in its research outputs, which have influenced global policies and practices in sustainable development. Dr. Louise Fresco, President of the Executive Board of WUR, emphasizes the role of research in driving sustainability: "At Wageningen, we believe that research is the key to unlocking sustainable solutions. Our work is not just about understanding the problems; it's about finding actionable solutions that can be implemented on a global scale."

WUR's research initiatives demonstrate how universities can lead in developing sustainable technologies and strategies. By engaging students in this research, WUR provides them with the opportunity to contribute to meaningful, impactful work that addresses some of the world's most pressing environmental challenges.

Leading by Example

The way educational institutions manage their campuses can serve as a powerful example of sustainability in action. By implementing sustainable practices in energy use, waste management, transportation, and food services, institutions can reduce their environmental impact and demonstrate their commitment to sustainability. These practices also provide opportunities for students to learn about sustainability in a practical, hands-on way.

Middlebury College in Vermont has made sustainability a central focus of its campus operations. The college's commitment to achieving carbon neutrality by 2016 was a bold move that required significant changes to its energy systems, waste management practices, and transportation policies. Middlebury's biomass heating plant, which uses locally sourced wood chips, is a key component of its sustainability efforts, reducing the college's reliance on fossil fuels and lowering its carbon footprint. Laurie Patton, President of Middlebury College, explains the importance of campus sustainability: "Sustainability is not just a goal; it's a practice that must be woven into the everyday operations of our campus. By leading by example, we show our students that sustainability is achievable and essential."

Middlebury's approach to campus sustainability highlights the importance of operational practices in promoting sustainability. By integrating sustainable practices into every aspect of campus life, the college creates a living model of sustainability for its students and the broader community.

Community Engagement and Outreach

Educational institutions have a responsibility not only to educate their students but also to engage with and support their surrounding communities. Through outreach programs, partnerships, and public engagement, institutions can extend their impact beyond the campus, promoting sustainability in the wider community and fostering a culture of environmental stewardship.

ATREE, based in Bangalore, India, is an example of an institution that combines education, research, and community engagement to promote sustainability. ATREE's work focuses on biodiversity conservation, sustainable development, and environmental governance. The institution actively involves local communities in its projects, ensuring that its research and conservation efforts are grounded in the needs and knowledge of those who are most affected by environmental issues. Dr. Sharachchandra Lele, a senior fellow at ATREE, emphasizes the importance of community engagement: "Sustainability cannot be achieved in isolation. It requires the active participation of communities who are directly impacted by environmental issues. At ATREE, we believe that by working together with local communities, we can create solutions that are not only effective but also equitable and sustainable."

ATREE's approach demonstrates how educational institutions can extend their impact by engaging with the communities around them. Through partnerships and outreach, ATREE ensures that its work contributes to both environmental sustainability and social equity.

Preparing Students for a Sustainable Future

Ultimately, the goal of integrating sustainability into education is to prepare students for a future where they will need to navigate complex environmental challenges and contribute to a more sustainable world. This preparation involves not only imparting knowledge but also fostering the skills, values, and mindsets needed to be effective change-makers.

The University of Gothenburg in Sweden has made sustainability a core focus of its educational mission. The university offers a wide range of programs and courses that emphasize sustainability, from environmental science to sustainable business practices. In addition to academic coursework, the university encourages students to engage in sustainability-related extracurricular activities, internships, and community projects. Eva Wiberg, Vice-Chancellor of the University of Gothenburg, discusses the importance of preparing students for a sustainable future: "Our students are the leaders of tomorrow, and it's our responsibility to ensure that they are equipped to address the environmental challenges they will face. By integrating sustainability into every aspect of their education, we empower them to make a positive impact in their careers and communities."

The University of Gothenburg's approach highlights the importance of a holistic education that goes beyond the classroom. By providing students with a well-rounded experience that includes academic learning, practical experience, and community engagement, the university prepares its graduates to be effective advocates for sustainability in their professional and personal lives.

Overcoming Challenges in Sustainability Education

While there are many success stories in sustainability education, there are also significant challenges that institutions must overcome. These challenges include limited resources, resistance to change, and the difficulty of integrating sustainability into established curricula and operations. Educational leaders must navigate these challenges with creativity and determination, finding ways to advance sustainability even in the face of obstacles.

The University of Cape Town has faced significant challenges in its efforts to promote sustainability, including resource constraints and the need to balance sustainability initiatives with other institutional priorities. Despite these challenges, UCT has made significant strides in integrating sustainability into its operations and academic offerings. The university's Green Campus Initiative, led by students, has been instrumental in driving sustainability on campus, from energy-saving measures to recycling programs. Professor Mamokgethi Phakeng, Vice-Chancellor of UCT, reflects on the challenges of sustainability education: "Sustainability is not always easy, but it is essential. At UCT, we have learned that by empowering our students and working together as a community, we can overcome obstacles and make meaningful progress toward a more sustainable future."

UCT's experience demonstrates that while the path to sustainability is not always straightforward, it is possible to make significant progress by engaging the entire campus community and maintaining a commitment to sustainability even in the face of challenges.

Sustainability and education are deeply interconnected, with educational institutions playing a crucial role in promoting sustainable practices and preparing students for a sustainable future. From integrating sustainability into the curriculum and campus operations to engaging with local communities and driving research and innovation, educational institutions have the power to lead by example and make a lasting impact on the world. While challenges remain, the commitment of these institutions to sustainability education offers hope for a future where education is a driving force for environmental stewardship and social equity. As educational leaders, the responsibility to advance sustainability is both a challenge and an opportunity. By embracing this responsibility with vision, creativity, and determination, we can ensure that our institutions not only contribute to a more sustainable world but also prepare our students to be the leaders and innovators who will shape that future.

As we look to the future, it is clear that the path to sustainability will require ongoing commitment, innovation, and collaboration. By working together, educational institutions can lead the way in creating a more just, equitable, and sustainable world for generations to come.

Key Takeaways

- Educational institutions have the power and responsibility to lead by example, embedding sustainability into their operations, curricula, and community engagement efforts. By doing so, they not only educate students but also demonstrate the practical application of sustainable practices.

- Sustainability is not confined to environmental science; it intersects with all fields of study. Institutions like the University of British Columbia show that by embedding sustainability across the curriculum, students from all disciplines can be equipped to contribute to a sustainable future.

- Universities are at the forefront of research and innovation in sustainability, developing new technologies and strategies that address global environmental challenges. Institutions like Wageningen University exemplify how research can drive practical solutions for a sustainable world.

- Sustainability efforts must extend beyond the campus. By engaging with local communities and stakeholders, institutions can foster a culture of sustainability that has a broader social impact. ATREE's work in India illustrates the importance of community involvement in achieving sustainable outcomes.

- The path to sustainability is not without challenges, including resource constraints and resistance to change. However, as demonstrated by the University of Cape Town, with creativity, determination, and a commitment to engaging the entire community, educational institutions can overcome obstacles and make meaningful progress toward sustainability.

CHAPTER XXV

The Future of Higher Education

*"The best way to predict the future is to create it. —
Peter Drucker"*

As we reach the end of this book, it's time to take a step back and reflect on the journey we've taken together. Higher education is standing on the brink of a transformative era. The forces shaping this change—technology, globalization, sustainability—are not just trends; they are profound shifts that will redefine the landscape of education for generations to come. This chapter is about looking forward, imagining what lies ahead, and considering how we, as educators, leaders, and learners, can navigate this future with purpose and vision.

Throughout this book, we've explored the many facets of higher education in the digital age. We've delved into how technology is reshaping learning environments, how sustainability is becoming a core mission for institutions, and how leadership must evolve to meet these new challenges. Each chapter has built upon the last, creating a tapestry of ideas, strategies, and visions for the future.

Now, as we conclude, it's important to connect these threads and consider how they come together to shape the future of higher education. This future isn't just about adopting new tools or policies; it's about reimagining what education can be in a world that is more connected, complex, and dynamic than ever before.

Emerging Trends Shaping the Future

The future of higher education is not a distant concept; it's unfolding right now, in classrooms, lecture halls, and online platforms around the world. Several key trends are driving this change, and understanding them is crucial for anyone involved in education today.

The Rise of Digital and Hybrid Learning Models

The acceleration of digital learning during the COVID-19 pandemic has permanently altered the educational landscape. Even as in-person classes resume, the flexibility and accessibility of online education have become integral to how we think about learning. Institutions like the Open University in the UK have been at the forefront of this shift, blending online and in-person learning to meet the diverse needs of students. Digital learning is no longer just a convenience; it's a necessity. As Dr. Tim Blackman, Vice-Chancellor of the Open University, puts it, "The future of education lies in flexibility and accessibility. By leveraging digital tools, we can provide a high-quality education to students regardless of their location or circumstances."

Personalization and Adaptive Learning Technologies

Another significant trend is the personalization of education through adaptive learning technologies. These technologies allow for a tailored educational experience, adjusting to the unique needs and learning styles of each student. Carnegie Mellon University's work in this area is leading the way, using AI to create personalized learning paths that help students succeed in ways that traditional models often cannot. "Education should not be one-size-fits-all," says Dr. Farnam Jahanian, President of Carnegie Mellon University. "By using adaptive technologies, we can create personalized learning pathways that help each student reach their full potential."

The Globalization of Higher Education

Higher education is becoming increasingly global. Universities are forming international partnerships, offering cross-border programs, and attracting students from all corners of the world. This globalization of education enriches learning experiences and prepares students for the interconnected world they will work in. The partnership between the University of Cape Town and Harvard University on global health challenges is a prime example of how institutions can collaborate to address global issues. "In today's interconnected world, collaboration is essential," says Professor Mamokgethi Phakeng, Vice-Chancellor of UCT. "Our partnership with Harvard allows us to pool our resources and expertise to tackle global challenges."

Lifelong Learning and the Changing Nature of Work

The traditional model of education, where one completes their studies early in life and then enters the workforce, is becoming obsolete. The National University of Singapore's Lifelong Learning Initiative reflects a broader shift towards continuous education, where individuals regularly upskill or reskill to keep pace with the changing demands of the job market. "The pace of change in today's world is unprecedented," says Professor Tan Eng Chye, President of NUS. "To keep up, individuals must be willing to learn and adapt throughout their lives."

The Role of Ethical Leadership in Navigating the Future

As we embrace the digital age, the ethical dimensions of education cannot be overlooked. Issues like data privacy, equity, and the potential for bias in AI-driven systems are becoming increasingly important. Stanford University's Ethical AI in Education Initiative, launched in 2024, addresses these challenges by setting standards for the ethical use of AI in educational settings. "As we embrace the potential of AI in education, we must also be vigilant in ensuring that these technologies are used ethically," says Dr. Marc Tessier-Lavigne, President of Stanford University. This kind of ethical leadership is crucial as we navigate the complexities of the digital age.

So, what does the future of higher education look like? Imagine a world where learning is truly personalized—where each student's educational journey is tailored to their strengths, interests, and needs. Picture a global network of institutions working together to solve the world's most pressing challenges, from climate change to global health. Envision universities that are not just places of learning but also hubs of innovation, sustainability, and ethical leadership.

This is a future where education is a lifelong journey, not just a phase of life. It's a future where higher education is accessible to all, regardless of geography, economic status, or background. And it's a future where the leaders of educational institutions are not just administrators, but visionaries who are committed to making the world a better place through education.

The future of higher education doesn't just happen; it is shaped by the decisions and actions of those who lead it. As you finish this book, think about the role you can play in bringing about this future. Whether you are a university administrator, a faculty member, or a policymaker, your leadership is crucial.

- Embrace innovation, foster inclusivity, and lead with a vision for the future. Implement new technologies, form global partnerships, and prioritize ethical practices. These actions will help ensure that your institution is not only prepared for the future but is also leading the way.
- Build networks with other educational leaders. Share insights, best practices, and support one another as you navigate the evolving landscape of higher education. By working together, we can create a community of practice that drives positive change.

As we look to the future, it's easy to focus on the challenges—the rapid pace of technological change, the uncertainties of a globalized world, the ethical dilemmas posed by new technologies. But it's also a time of incredible opportunity. The future of higher education is bright, filled with the potential to transform lives, societies, and the world.

- The future of higher education is filled with possibilities. By embracing the challenges and opportunities of the digital age, we can create a future where education is more inclusive, equitable, and innovative than ever before. This is a future where students are empowered to succeed and to shape the world around them.

- Stay engaged with the ongoing conversation about the future of higher education. Whether through further reading, participation in forums, or contributing your ideas and leadership, your involvement is vital to the continued evolution of education.

As you move forward from this book, carry with you the knowledge, insights, and inspiration that have been shared. The future of higher education is not predetermined; it is shaped by the actions and decisions of those who lead it. As an educational leader, you have the power to influence this future—to make it one that is brighter, more just, and more hopeful.

> *"In the words of Nelson Mandela, "Education is the most powerful weapon which you can use to change the world." Let this be your guiding principle as you continue your journey as a leader in higher education."*

It is clear that the future of education is filled with both promise and uncertainty. But with visionary leadership, a commitment to ethical principles, and a willingness to embrace change, we can ensure that higher education remains a force for good in the world.

Thank you for embarking on this journey. The path ahead is not easy, but it is filled with possibilities. As you continue your work, may you be inspired to lead with courage, innovation, and a deep commitment to the values that make education such a powerful and transformative force in society.

Key Takeaways

- The future of higher education lies in adopting flexible learning models that blend digital and in-person experiences, making education more accessible and adaptable to diverse student needs.
- As education evolves, the use of adaptive learning technologies will be crucial in providing personalized learning experiences that cater to the individual needs and strengths of each student.
- The globalization of higher education offers new opportunities for collaboration and knowledge exchange, enabling institutions to tackle global challenges through innovative partnerships.
- In a rapidly changing job market, the concept of lifelong learning will become increasingly important, requiring educational institutions to offer continuous learning opportunities that allow individuals to upskill and reskill throughout their careers.
- As technology becomes more integrated into education, ethical leadership will be essential in ensuring that advancements like AI are used responsibly, prioritizing equity, fairness, and the well-being of students.

Notes

Chapter 1: The Digital Revolution in Education

- *National Education Policy 2020.* Available at: https://www.education.gov.in/sites/upload_files/mhrd/files/NEP_Final_English_0.pdf
- *Eneza Education Impact Report 2024.* Available at: https://enezaeducation.com
- *E-Learning in Africa: Opportunities and Challenges.* Available at: https://www.worldbank.org/en/news/feature/2021/04/15/e-learning-in-africa-opportunities-and-challenges
- *Internet Plus Education Initiative: Progress Report.* Available at: http://en.moe.gov.cn/
- *Education in Rural China: Addressing the Digital Divide.* Available at: https://unesdoc.unesco.org/ark:/48223/pf0000373277
- *Digital Pedagogy and Continuous Professional Development for Teachers.* Available at: https://www.oph.fi/en
- *The Role of Educators in the Digital Age.* Finnish National Agency for Education. Available at: https://www.oph.fi/en/articles/role-educators-digital-age
- *Smart Nation and Digital Government Office: Education Initiatives.* Available at: https://www.smartnation.gov.sg/what-is-smart-nation/initiatives/Education

- *Navigating the Future: Singapore's Approach to Digital Education Leadership.* Available at: https://www.moe.gov.sg

Chapter 2: Digital Leadership in the Age of Transformation

- *Digital Leadership and Innovation in Danish Education.* Available at: https://www.ncde.dk
- *Digital Literacy Initiative: Equipping Leaders for the Future.* Available at: https://www.unimelb.edu.au
- *Smart Education 2.0: Strategic Vision and Implementation.* Available at: http://english.moe.go.kr
- *Managing Digital Transformation in Traditional Educational Settings.* Available at: https://www.keio.ac.jp/en/
- *Strategies for Digital Innovation in Japanese Education.* Available at: https://www.mext.go.jp/en/
- *Collaborative Leadership in Digital Education: A Case Study.* Available at: http://www.open.ac.uk
- *Innovation Lab: Pioneering Digital Transformation in South African Education.* Available at: https://www.uct.ac.za
- *Leadership Development and the Growth Mindset in a Digital World.* Available at: https://www.ntu.edu.sg
- *Digital Learning Strategy: Prioritizing Diversity and Inclusion.* Available at: https://www.ubc.ca

Chapter 3: Strategic Vision and Agile Planning for Digital Transformation

- *Digital 2025: Strategic Vision for a Digital Future.* Available at: https://www.sydney.edu.au
- *Leading the Digital Transformation at the University of Sydney.* Available at: https://www.sydney.edu.au
- *Vision 2030: Shaping the Future of Education and Research through Digital Transformation.* Available at: https://www.iitb.ac.in
- *Innovating for the Future: IIT Bombay's Strategic Vision.* Available at: https://www.iitb.ac.in
- *Agile Planning in Education: The NUS Digital Transformation Framework.* Available at: https://www.nus.edu.sg
- *Staying Ahead in the Digital Age: Agile Planning at NUS.* Available at: https://www.nus.edu.sg
- *Digital UCL: A Strategic Framework for Digital Transformation.* Available at: https://www.ucl.ac.uk
- *Turning Vision into Reality: The Execution of Digital UCL Strategy.* Available at: https://www.ucl.ac.uk
- *Navigating Resistance: ETH Zurich's Strategy for Digital Transformation.* Available at: https://ethz.ch/en.html
- Springman, S. (2024). *Digital Transformation at ETH Zurich: Overcoming Challenges and Embracing Innovation.* Available at: https://ethz.ch/en.html
- *Leading Digital Transformation in Latin America: The PUC Chile Strategy.* Available at: https://www.uc.cl
- *Visionary Leadership in Digital Education: Insights from PUC Chile.* Available at: https://www.uc.cl

Chapter 4: Change Management in Digital Education

- *Managing Digital Transformation: Strategies for Faculty Engagement and Collaboration.* Available at: https://www.univie.ac.at/en/
- *Faculty Forums on Digital Transformation: Building Collaboration and Reducing Resistance.* Available at: https://www.univie.ac.at/en/news/
- *Empowering Leadership at Every Level: SJTU's Digital Transformation Strategy.* Available at: http://en.sjtu.edu.cn/
- *The Role of Distributed Leadership in Digital Transformation at SJTU.* Available at: http://en.sjtu.edu.cn/leadership/
- *Fostering Innovation: Lund University's Approach to Digital Transformation.* Available at: https://www.lu.se/en/
- *Creating a Culture of Innovation in Higher Education: Insights from Lund University.* Available at: https://www.lu.se/en/leadership/
- University of Cape Town. (2023). *Collaborative Change Management in Digital Transformation: A Case Study from UCT.* Available at: https://www.uct.ac.za/
- *The Power of Collaboration in Overcoming Resistance to Digital Change.* Available at: https://www.uct.ac.za/leadership/
- *Supporting Faculty through Digital Transformation: UBC's Approach.* Available at: https://www.ubc.ca/
- *Investing in Success: The Role of Support in Digital Transformation at UBC.* Available at: https://www.ubc.ca/president/

- *Sustaining Digital Transformation through Continuous Improvement: The Auckland Model.* Available at: https://www.auckland.ac.nz/
- *Continuous Improvement in Digital Education: Lessons from the University of Auckland.* Available at: https://www.auckland.ac.nz/leadership/

Chapter 5: Innovative Teaching Models in the Digital Age

- *A-VIEW: Blended Learning at Amrita University.* Available at: https://www.amrita.edu/
- *Enhancing Education through Blended Learning: Insights from Amrita University.* Available at: https://www.amrita.edu/leadership/
- *Hybrid Learning at The Open University: Flexibility and Accessibility in Higher Education.* Available at: https://www.open.ac.uk/
- *Innovative Learning: The Role of Hybrid Models at The Open University.* Available at: https://www.open.ac.uk/about/teaching/
- *The Flipped Classroom Model at SMU: Maximizing In-Class Engagement.* Available at: https://www.smu.edu.sg/
- *Transforming Education with the Flipped Classroom: A SMU Case Study.* Available at: https://www.smu.edu.sg/leadership/
- *Gamification in Education: Enhancing Learning at the University of Helsinki.* Available at: https://www.helsinki.fi/en
- *The Power of Gamification: Engaging Students through*

Game-Based Learning. Available at: https://www.helsinki.fi/en/faculty/

- *Problem-Based Learning at Aalto: Preparing Students for Real-World Challenges.* Available at: https://www.aalto.fi/en
- *Innovative Pedagogy: Problem-Based Learning at Aalto University.* Available at: https://www.aalto.fi/en/leadership/
- *AI in Education: Personalizing Learning at the University of Tokyo.* Available at: https://www.u-tokyo.ac.jp/en/
- *Harnessing AI for Personalized Education: A Case Study from the University of Tokyo.* Available at: https://www.u-tokyo.ac.jp/en/research/
- *Exploring the Potential of Virtual Reality in Education: The UvA Experience.* Available at: https://www.uva.nl/en
- *Virtual Reality in Education: Innovations at the University of Amsterdam.* Available at: https://www.uva.nl/en/research/
- *Bringing Education to Underserved Communities through Blended Learning.* Available at: https://www.bridgeinternationalacademies.com/
- *Making Education Accessible: The Role of Blended Learning at Bridge International Academies.* Available at: https://www.bridgeinternationalacademies.com/about/
- *Hybrid Learning for Adult Learners: Innovations at Oulu University of Applied Sciences.* Available at: https://www.oamk.fi/en/
- *Expanding Access to Education through Hybrid Learning: Insights from Oulu University of Applied Sciences.* Available at: https://www.oamk.fi/en/about-oamk/

Chapter 6: Engagement and Motivation in Digital Learning

- *Gamified Learning Modules: Transforming Education through Digital Innovation.* Available at: https://www.nalandauniv.edu.in/
- *The Role of Gamification in Enhancing Student Engagement at Nalanda University.* Available at: https://www.nalandauniv.edu.in/leadership/
- *Virtual Labs in Science and Engineering: Expanding Access to Practical Learning.* Available at: https://www.unimelb.edu.au/
- *Enhancing STEM Education through Virtual Laboratories at the University of Melbourne.* Available at: https://www.unimelb.edu.au/science/
- *Building a Culture of Engagement through Digital Collaboration: A Case Study from SNU.* Available at: http://en.snu.ac.kr/
- *Fostering Student Collaboration in Digital Learning Environments at Seoul National University.* Available at: http://en.snu.ac.kr/leadership/
- *Personalizing Learning with AI: Innovations in Digital Education at Edinburgh.* Available at: https://www.ed.ac.uk/
- *The Impact of AI on Student Engagement and Motivation at the University of Edinburgh.* Available at: https://www.ed.ac.uk/research/
- *Ensuring Success in Digital Learning: The Role of Digital Literacy at OUHK.* Available at: https://www.ouhk.edu.hk/
- *Promoting Digital Literacy for Effective Engagement in Online Learning at OUHK.* Available at:

https://www.ouhk.edu.hk/leadership/
- *Bridging Educational Gaps with Gamification: A Rural Education Initiative in Colombia.* Available at: https://uniandes.edu.co/en
- *Gamified Education in Rural Colombia: The Impact on Student Engagement at Universidad de los Andes.* Available at: https://uniandes.edu.co/en/about/

Chapter 7: Building the Digital Foundation: Technology Integration and Infrastructure

- *Digital Infrastructure Overhaul at the University of Tokyo.* Available at: https://www.u-tokyo.ac.jp/en/
- *The Importance of Strong Digital Infrastructure in Modern Education.* Available at: https://www.u-tokyo.ac.jp/en/about/leadership/
- *Future Classroom Initiative: Integrating Technology into Education.* Available at: https://www.utu.fi/en
- *Digital Natives and the Integration of Technology in Education.* Available at: https://www.utu.fi/en/research/
- *Challenges and Successes in Digital Infrastructure Upgrades at UCT.* Available at: https://www.uct.ac.za/
- *Navigating the Complexities of Digital Transformation in Higher Education.* Available at: https://www.uct.ac.za/about/leadership/
- *Advanced Cybersecurity Measures at ETH Zurich.* Available at: https://ethz.ch/en.html
- *Proactive Cybersecurity: Ensuring a Secure Digital Campus.* Available at: https://ethz.ch/en/about/leadership.html

- *Sustainable Digital Infrastructure: NUS's Green IT Initiative.* Available at: https://www.nus.edu.sg/
- *Building a Sustainable and Scalable Digital Foundation at NUS.* Available at: https://www.nus.edu.sg/about/leadership
- *Exploring Quantum Computing in Education: MIT's New Initiative.* Available at: https://www.mit.edu/
- *Quantum Computing and the Future of Digital Infrastructure in Education.* Available at: https://www.mit.edu/about/leadership

Chapter 8: Digital Equity and Inclusion

- *Pradhan Mantri Gramin Digital Saksharta Abhiyan (PMGDISHA) Overview.* Available at: https://pmgdisha.in
- *Individuals Using the Internet (% of Population).* Available at: https://data.worldbank.org/indicator/IT.NET.USER.ZS
- *Bridging the Homework Gap through Broadband Access.* Available at: https://www.fcc.gov/reports-research/working-papers/bridging-homework-gap-through-broadband-access
- *ASEAN Digital Masterplan 2025.* Available at: https://asean.org/wp-content/uploads/2021/01/ASEAN-Digital-Masterplan-2025.pdf
- *NBN Co Corporate Plan 2021-24.* Available at: https://www.nbnco.com.au
- *Digital Literacy Programme (DLP) Overview.* Available at: http://www.icta.go.ke/dlp/
- *Digitalization and Digital Inclusion in Finnish Education.*

Available at: https://www.oph.fi/en
- *Digital Education Action Plan (2021-2027)*. Available at: https://ec.europa.eu/education/education-in-the-eu/digital-education-action-plan_en

Chapter 9: Data-Driven Decision Making in Education

- *National Assessment Program - Literacy and Numeracy (NAPLAN)*. Available at: https://www.nap.edu.au
- *Data Integration and Management Systems Overview*. Available at: https://achieve.lausd.net
- *Code of Practice for Learning Analytics*. Available at: https://www.jisc.ac.uk/guides/code-of-practice-for-learning-analytics
- Ministry of Education, Singapore. (2020). *Education Statistics Digest 2020*. Available at: https://www.moe.gov.sg/docs/default-source/document/publications/education-statistics-
- *DIKSHA - Digital Infrastructure for Knowledge Sharing*. Available at: https://diksha.gov.in
- *AI in Education: Transforming Learning through Technology*. Available at: https://www.tal.com
- *Artificial Intelligence in Education*. Available at: https://www.squirrelai.com
- *General Data Protection Regulation (GDPR)*. Available at: https://gdpr.eu

Chapter 10: Professional Development for Digital Competence

- *Digital Badge Initiative for Online Teaching.* Available at: https://www.teachingandlearning.ie/
- *Digital Teaching Academy Overview.* Available at: https://www.u-tokyo.ac.jp/en/education/digital_teaching_academy.html
- *Ethics and Data Privacy in Digital Education: Professional Development Programs.* Available at: https://www.ku.dk/english/
- *Technology-Enhanced Learning (TEL) Program Report.* Available at: https://www.nie.edu.sg/
- *National Digital Library of India (NDLI): Expanding Access to Professional Development.* Available at: https://ndl.iitkgp.ac.in/
- *Digital Education Action Plan 2021-2027: Supporting Educators' Digital Competence.* Available at: https://ec.europa.eu/education/education-in-the-eu/digital-education-action-plan_en

Chapter 11: Cybersecurity and Data Privacy in Education

- *UCSF Statement on Ransomware Attack.* Available at: https://www.ucsf.edu
- *Data Breach Incident Report and Response Measures.* Available at: https://warwick.ac.uk
- *National Cybersecurity Strategy for Universities.* Available at: https://www.kisa.or.kr/eng/

- *General Data Protection Regulation (GDPR) Overview.* Available at: https://gdpr.eu
- *GDPR Compliance in Higher Education Institutions.* Available at: https://edpb.europa.eu
- *Cybersecurity Awareness Initiative.* Available at: https://www.uq.edu.au
- *Data Privacy Initiative and Policy.* Available at: https://www.iitb.ac.in
- *Cybersecurity and Data Privacy Course Description.* Available at: https://www.helsinki.fi/en

Chapter 12: E-Learning and Distance Education

- *IGNOU's New AI-Driven E-Learning Platform: Expanding Access to Education.* Available at: http://www.ignou.ac.in/
- *Democratizing Education through Technology at IGNOU.* Available at: http://www.ignou.ac.in/about/leadership/
- *Bridging the Digital Divide: UPOU's Initiative to Support Remote Learners.* Available at: https://www.upou.edu.ph/
- *Inclusivity in E-Learning: Addressing the Digital Divide at UPOU.* Available at: https://www.upou.edu.ph/about/leadership/
- *Innovations in Distance Education: Enhancing Student Engagement at The Open University.* Available at: http://www.open.ac.uk/
- *Using AI to Foster Student Engagement in Online Learning at The Open University.* Available at:

http://www.open.ac.uk/about/leadership

- *Quality Assurance and Academic Integrity in Online Education at USQ.* Available at: https://www.usq.edu.au/
- *Maintaining High Standards in E-Learning: USQ's Approach.* Available at: https://www.usq.edu.au/about/leadership
- *Globalizing Education: Expanding Access through Online Master's Programs at The University of Edinburgh.* Available at: https://www.ed.ac.uk/
- *Creating a Global Classroom: The Impact of E-Learning at The University of Edinburgh.* Available at: https://www.ed.ac.uk/about/leadership
- *NTU Learn+: Innovating E-Learning with AI and Gamification.* Available at: https://www.ntu.edu.sg/
- *Reimagining Education with Technology at NTU.* Available at: https://www.ntu.edu.sg/about/leadership
- *Lifelong Learning in the Digital Age: Online Courses for Professionals at The University of Helsinki.* Available at: https://www.helsinki.fi/en
- *Supporting Lifelong Learning through E-Learning at The University of Helsinki.* Available at: https://www.helsinki.fi/en/about/leadership

Chapter 13: Leadership in Times of Crisis

- *UCT's Response to the COVID-19 Crisis: Ensuring Equity in Access to Education.* Available at: https://www.uct.ac.za/
- *Leading Through Crisis: Reflections on UCT's Pandemic Response.* Available at: https://www.uct.ac.za/about/

leadership/

- *The NUS Resilience Initiative: Digital Transformation in Response to COVID-19.* Available at: https://www.nus.edu.sg/
- *Building a Resilient University: Insights from NUS's Response to the Pandemic.* Available at: https://www.nus.edu.sg/about/leadership
- *Mental Health and Well-Being During the Pandemic: The University of Melbourne's Approach.* Available at: https://www.unimelb.edu.au/
- *Caring for Our Community: The University of Melbourne's Wellness Initiatives During COVID-19.* Available at: https://about.unimelb.edu.au/leadership
- *Innovating in a Crisis: Universidad de los Andes' Response to the Pandemic.* Available at: https://uniandes.edu.co/en
- *Educational Innovation in Times of Crisis: Lessons from Universidad de los Andes.* Available at: https://uniandes.edu.co/en/about/leadership
- *Transforming Tradition: How Oxford Adapted to the COVID-19 Pandemic.* Available at: https://www.ox.ac.uk/
- *The Long-Term Impact of the Pandemic on Educational Leadership at Oxford.* Available at: https://www.ox.ac.uk/about/organisation/university-officers/vice-chancellor

Chapter 14: Global Trends in Education

- *JNU's Global Collaborations: Strengthening International Partnerships.* Available at: https://www.jnu.ac.in/

- *Globalizing Education: Reflections from JNU.* Available at: https://www.jnu.ac.in/about/leadership/
- *UCT and Humboldt University Collaboration on Climate Change.* Available at: https://www.uct.ac.za/
- *Global Partnerships in Education: Humboldt and UCT's Joint Initiatives.* Available at: https://www.hu-berlin.de/en/
- *Global Classroom: Tokyo's Initiative for International Online Learning.* Available at: https://www.u-tokyo.ac.jp/en/
- *The Future of Education: A Global Classroom Experience.* Available at: https://www.u-tokyo.ac.jp/en/about/leadership/
- *Educating Ethical Leaders: Ashesi's Global Curriculum.* Available at: https://www.ashesi.edu.gh/
- *Building Global Leaders: The Ashesi Approach to Education.* Available at: https://www.ashesi.edu.gh/about/leadership/
- *Balancing Global Engagement with Cultural Preservation: Tsinghua's Strategy.* Available at: https://www.tsinghua.edu.cn/en/
- *Navigating Globalization: Insights from Tsinghua University.* Available at: https://www.tsinghua.edu.cn/en/about/leadership/
- *Global Leadership Program: Preparing Educational Leaders for a Globalized World.* Available at: https://www.sydney.edu.au/
- *Leading in a Globalized World: The University of Sydney's Leadership Development Strategy.* Available at: https://www.sydney.edu.au/about/leadership

Chapter 15: Building a Culture of Innovation

- *Embracing Innovation: Amity's Journey in Integrating Advanced Technologies in Education.* Available at: https://www.amity.edu/
- *Innovation as a Core Value at Amity University.* Available at: https://www.amity.edu/about/leadership/
- *The d.school Approach: Fostering Creativity and Innovation through Design Thinking.* Available at: https://www.stanford.edu/
- *Encouraging Experimentation: Stanford's Culture of Innovation.* Available at: https://dschool.stanford.edu/about
- *NTU's Integration of AI and Virtual Learning in Education.* Available at: https://www.ntu.edu.sg/
- *Technology as an Enabler of Learning: Insights from NTU.* Available at: https://www.ntu.edu.sg/about/leadership
- *The Innovation Hub: Collaboration and Inclusivity at UCT.* Available at: https://www.uct.ac.za/
- *Driving Innovation through Collaboration: The UCT Experience.* Available at: https://www.uct.ac.za/about/leadership
- *Continuous Improvement and Innovation in Education at Helsinki.* Available at: https://www.helsinki.fi/en
- *A Commitment to Lifelong Learning: How Helsinki Embraces Continuous Improvement.* Available at: https://www.helsinki.fi/en/about/leadership

Chapter 16: The Role of Artificial Intelligence in Education

- *LearnX: Personalizing Education Through AI at Ashoka.* Available at: https://www.ashoka.edu.in/
- *AI in Education: Transforming Learning at Ashoka University.* Available at: https://www.ashoka.edu.in/about/leadership/
- *EdAI: Enhancing Student Services Through AI.* Available at: https://www.ed.ac.uk/
- *AI in Administration: The Impact of EdAI at the University of Edinburgh.* Available at: https://www.ed.ac.uk/about/leadership
- *SmartLearn: AI-Powered Personalized Learning at UNSW.* Available at: https://www.unsw.edu.au/
- *The Future of Personalized Learning: AI at UNSW.* Available at: https://www.unsw.edu.au/about/leadership
- *Ethics in AI: Addressing Bias and Privacy at IIT Bombay.* Available at: https://www.iitb.ac.in/
- *Ensuring Ethical AI in Education: Insights from IIT Bombay.* Available at: https://www.iitb.ac.in/en/about/leadership
- *TeachAI: Supporting Educators with AI at McMaster.* Available at: https://www.mcmaster.ca/
- *AI as a Partner in Teaching: McMaster University's Approach.* Available at: https://www.mcmaster.ca/about/leadership

Chapter 17: Student-Centered Leadership in the Digital Age

- *Student Advisory Councils: Enhancing Student Voice at UQ.* Available at: https://www.uq.edu.au/
- *Student-Centered Leadership at UQ: Listening and Learning from Our Students.* Available at: https://www.uq.edu.au/about/leadership
- *Amrita Engage: Personalized Learning through AI.* Available at: https://www.amrita.edu/
- *Engaging Students with Digital Tools: Insights from Amrita.* Available at: https://www.amrita.edu/about/leadership
- *The Student Success Collaborative: Using Data to Support Students.* Available at: https://www.asu.edu/
- *Data-Driven Leadership at ASU: Creating Success through Insights.* Available at: https://www.asu.edu/about/leadership
- *Balancing Technology and Personal Connection: UCT's Student Success Program.* Available at: https://www.uct.ac.za/
- *The Human Element in a Digital World: UCT's Approach to Student Support.* Available at: https://www.uct.ac.za/about/leadership
- *Digital Accessibility at the Open University: Making Education Inclusive.* Available at: https://www.open.ac.uk/
- *Creating an Accessible Learning Environment: The Open University's Mission.* Available at: https://www.open.ac.uk/about/leadership

Chapter 18: Curriculum Design for the Future

- *Digital Ready: Integrating Digital Literacy Across All Levels.* Available at: https://www.moe.gov.sg/
- *The Future of Digital Literacy in Singapore's Education System.* Available at: https://www.moe.gov.sg/about-us/leadership
- *Critical Thinking and Inquiry-Based Learning at Ashesi.* Available at: https://www.ashesi.edu.gh/
- *Building Ethical Leaders Through Critical Thinking: Ashesi University's Approach.* Available at: https://www.ashesi.edu.gh/about/leadership
- *Interdisciplinary Education at JGU: Preparing Students for Global Challenges.* Available at: https://jgu.edu.in/
- *The Importance of Interdisciplinary Studies in Addressing Global Issues.* Available at: https://jgu.edu.in/about/leadership/
- *Developing Soft Skills and Emotional Intelligence Through Experiential Learning.* Available at: https://www.aalto.fi/en
- *Why Soft Skills Matter in the Digital Age: Aalto University's Perspective.* Available at: https://www.aalto.fi/en/about/leadership
- *Tsinghua Lifelong Learning Program: Continuous Education for a Changing World.* Available at: https://www.tsinghua.edu.cn/en/
- *The Role of Lifelong Learning in Maintaining Professional Relevance.* Available at: https://www.tsinghua.edu.cn/en/about/leadership

Chapter 19: Ethics and Digital Responsibility in Education

- *Digital Citizenship Education in Finland: Integrating Ethical Use of Technology into the Curriculum.* Available at: https://www.oph.fi/en
- *The Importance of Digital Citizenship in Finnish Education.* Available at: https://www.oph.fi/en/about-us/leadership
- *Digital Ethics Program at UCT: Preparing Students for the Digital World.* Available at: https://www.uct.ac.za/
- *Ethical Online Behavior and Education at UCT.* Available at: https://www.uct.ac.za/about/leadership
- *Ethics in Digital Education: Guidelines and Policies at IIT Delhi.* Available at: https://home.iitd.ac.in/
- *Leadership and Ethical Technology Use in Education.* Available at: https://home.iitd.ac.in/about/leadership
- *Bridging the Digital Divide: The Impact of Kenya's Digital Literacy Program.* Available at: https://www.education.go.ke/
- *Digital Equity and Education: Kenya's Approach to Inclusive Technology.* Available at: https://www.education.go.ke/about/leadership
- *AI Ethics in Education: Guidelines from the University of Edinburgh.* Available at: https://www.ed.ac.uk/
- *Ensuring Ethical AI Use in Education.* Available at: https://www.ed.ac.uk/about/leadership

Chapter 20: The Role of EdTech Companies in Shaping the Future of Education

- *Empowering Working Professionals Through Online Education.* Available at: https://www.upgrad.com/
- *upGrad's Mission to Make Education Accessible and Relevant for Professionals.* Available at: https://www.upgrad.com/about/leadership
- *Partnering with Universities to Expand Access to Education Globally.* Available at: https://www.coursera.org/
- *The Transformative Power of Educational Partnerships on a Global Scale.* Available at: https://www.coursera.org/about/leadership
- *Providing Free, World-Class Education for Anyone, Anywhere.* Available at: https://www.khanacademy.org/
- *The Importance of Accessibility in Education: Khan Academy's Vision.* Available at: https://www.khanacademy.org/about/leadership
- *Reimagining Higher Education Through Technology and Active Learning.* Available at: https://www.minerva.kgi.edu/
- *The Role of Educational Leadership in a Technology-Driven Learning Environment.* Available at: https://www.minerva.kgi.edu/about/leadership
- *Transforming Education for Competitive Exams Through Technology.* Available at: https://unacademy.com/
- *The Future of EdTech: Personalizing Learning Through AI and Technology.* Available at: https://unacademy.com/about/leadership

Chapter 21: Leading Educational Change

- *Early Childhood Education in Finland: A Comprehensive Approach to Child Development.* Available at: https://www.oph.fi/en
- *The Role of Leadership in Transforming Early Childhood Education in Finland.* Available at: https://www.minedu.fi/en
- *SMART Education Initiative: A New Era of Digital Learning in South Korea.* Available at: http://english.moe.go.kr/
- *Leadership in Digital Transformation: Lessons from South Korea's Education System.* Available at: http://english.moe.go.kr/about/leadership
- *The Impact of the Nine-Year and Twelve-Year Basic Education Programs in Rwanda.* Available at: http://mineduc.gov.rw/
- *Driving Educational Change in Rwanda: A Focus on Inclusivity and Innovation.* Available at: http://mineduc.gov.rw/about/leadership
- *Indigenous-Led Education: Revitalizing Cultures Through Learning.* Available at: https://www.fnuniv.ca/
- *The Role of Leadership in Indigenous Education: Insights from First Nations University of Canada.* Available at: https://www.fnuniv.ca/about/leadership
- *New Pathways Initiative: Transforming Vocational Education in Brazil.* Available at: http://portal.mec.gov.br/
- *Aligning Education with Labor Market Needs: Brazil's Vocational Education Reforms.* Available at: http://portal.mec.gov.br/about/leadership

Chapter 22: Future-Ready Skills and Competencies

- *Building a Future-Ready Workforce Through Reskilling and Digital Training.* Available at: https://www.infosys.com/
- *The Importance of Lifelong Learning and Adaptability in the Digital Age.* Available at: https://www.infosys.com/about/leadership
- *Global Science Campus: Fostering Critical Thinking and Innovation in Education.* Available at: https://www.u-tokyo.ac.jp/en/
- *Navigating Complexity: The Role of Critical Thinking in Modern Education.* Available at: https://www.u-tokyo.ac.jp/about/leadership
- *Enhancing Emotional Intelligence and Interpersonal Skills in the Workforce.* Available at: https://www.hrdf.com.my/
- *The Role of Emotional Intelligence in Future Workplaces.* Available at: https://www.hrdf.com.my/about/leadership
- *Digital Learning Program: Preparing Students for the Future of Technology.* Available at: https://www.kaust.edu.sa/
- *The Critical Role of Digital Literacy in the 21st Century.* Available at: https://www.kaust.edu.sa/about/leadership
- *Design Factory: Fostering Creativity and Innovation in Education.* Available at: https://www.aalto.fi/en
- *Why Creativity is Essential for Future-Ready Graduates.* Available at: https://www.aalto.fi/en/about/leadership

- *Lifelong Learning Initiative: Empowering Students and Alumni to Stay Competitive.* Available at: https://www.nus.edu.sg/
- *Adapting to a Changing World: The Importance of Lifelong Learning.* Available at: https://www.nus.edu.sg/about/leadership
- *Global Leadership Program: Preparing Students for a Connected World.* Available at: https://unu.edu/
- *Global Competence as a Key to Success in an Interconnected World.* Available at: https://unu.edu/about/leadership
- *Young India Fellowship: Cultivating Ethical Leadership and Social Responsibility.* Available at: https://www.ashoka.edu.in/
- *The Role of Ethical Leadership in Shaping the Future of Society.* Available at: https://www.ashoka.edu.in/about/leadership

Chapter 23: Governance and Policy in the Digital Age

- *Digital Nation: How Estonia Leads the World in E-Governance.* Available at: https://e-estonia.com/
- *The Role of Digital Governance in Modern Education Systems.* Available at: https://president.ee/en/
- *National Education Policy 2020: Bridging the Digital Divide.* Available at: https://www.education.gov.in/
- *Equity in the Digital Age: Insights from India's NEP 2020.* Available at: https://www.education.gov.in/about/leadership
- *GDPR and Education: Ensuring Data Privacy in the Digital*

- *Age.* Available at: https://ec.europa.eu/info/law/law-topic/data-protection_en
- *Data Privacy in Education: The Importance of GDPR Compliance.* Available at: https://ec.europa.eu/commission/commissioners/2019-2024/ansip_en
- *Transforming Education through Smart Nation Policies.* Available at: https://www.smartnation.gov.sg/
- *Policy Innovation for the Digital Age: Singapore's Smart Nation Framework.* Available at: https://www.smartnation.gov.sg/about/leadership
- *Ethical AI in Education: Guidelines for Responsible Use.* Available at: https://en.unesco.org/themes/ethics-education
- *Navigating Ethical Challenges in Digital Education: UNESCO's Guidelines on AI.* Available at: https://en.unesco.org/about/leadership
- *Preparing Leaders for the Digital Age: The Digital Leadership Framework at Harvard.* Available at: https://www.harvard.edu/
- *Shaping the Future: Digital Leadership in Higher Education.* Available at: https://www.harvard.edu/about/leadership

Chapter 24: Sustainability and Education

- *Sustainability Education and Campus Initiatives.* Available at: https://www.terisas.ac.in/
- *Living Sustainability: The Role of Practice in Education.* Available at: https://www.terisas.ac.in/about/leadership
- *UBC Sustainability Initiative: Integrating Sustainability*

Across the Curriculum. Available at: https://sustain.ubc.ca/
- *Interdisciplinary Learning for a Sustainable Future.* Available at: https://www.ubc.ca/about/leadership
- *Sustainable Agriculture and Environmental Research.* Available at: https://www.wur.nl/en.htm
- *Research as a Key to Sustainable Solutions.* Available at: https://www.wur.nl/en/About-Wageningen/Board.htm
- *Achieving Carbon Neutrality: Middlebury's Sustainability Journey.* Available at: http://www.middlebury.edu/sustainability
- *Sustainability as a Practice in Campus Operations.* Available at: http://www.middlebury.edu/about/president
- *Community-Driven Sustainability: Engaging Local Communities in Environmental Stewardship.* Available at: https://www.atree.org/
- *The Importance of Community Engagement in Sustainability.* Available at: https://www.atree.org/about/leadership
- *Sustainability Education and Student Engagement.* Available at: https://www.gu.se/en
- *Preparing Students for a Sustainable Future.* Available at: https://www.gu.se/en/about/leadership
- *Green Campus Initiative: Student-Led Sustainability at UCT.* Available at: http://www.uct.ac.za/about/sustainability
- *Navigating the Challenges of Sustainability in Higher Education.* Available at: http://www.uct.ac.za/about/leadership

Chapter 25: The Future of Higher Education

- *Innovations in Hybrid Learning: Blending Online and In-Person Education.* Available at: https://www.open.ac.uk/
- Blackman, T. (2024). *Flexibility and Accessibility in the Future of Education.* Available at: https://www.open.ac.uk/about/leadership
- *Adaptive Learning Technologies at CMU: Personalizing Education Through AI.* Available at: https://www.cmu.edu/
- *The Role of AI in Personalizing Education.* Available at: https://www.cmu.edu/about/leadership
- *Global Partnerships in Education: The UCT-Harvard Collaboration on Global Health.* Available at: http://www.uct.ac.za/
- *The Importance of Global Collaboration in Higher Education.* Available at: http://www.uct.ac.za/about/leadership
- *Lifelong Learning at NUS: Adapting to the Changing Nature of Work.* Available at: https://nus.edu.sg/
- *The Future of Lifelong Learning and Its Impact on Education.* Available at: https://nus.edu.sg/about/leadership
- *Ethical AI in Education: Addressing the Challenges of the Digital Age.* Available at: https://www.stanford.edu/
- *Ethical Leadership in the Digital Age: The Role of AI in Education.* Available at: https://www.stanford.edu/about/leadership
- *Sustainability in Higher Education: The University of Tasmania's Commitment to Carbon Neutrality.* Available at: https://www.utas.edu.au/

- *Sustainability Leadership in Higher Education.* Available at: https://www.utas.edu.au/about/leadership
- *The Melbourne Leadership Academy: Preparing Future Educational Leaders.* Available at: https://www.unimelb.edu.au/
- *Innovative Leadership in Higher Education: The Melbourne Approach.* Available at: https://www.unimelb.edu.au/about/leadership
- *AI and Automation in Education: HKUST's Vision for the Future.* Available at: https://hkust.edu.hk/
- *The Impact of AI on the Future of Higher Education.* Available at: https://hkust.edu.hk/about/leadership

Portfolio

Anish K Ravi has carved a distinctive path across both corporate and academic landscapes, combining strategic insight with a passion for innovation and growth. As an accomplished author of three seminal books on marketing, he brings fresh, practical perspectives to the evolving challenges of the digital era, challenging conventional norms and inspiring new ways of thinking. Anish's work spans writing, teaching, consulting, and mentoring, all driven by a commitment to lifelong learning and a desire to empower others. His career reflects a dedication to fostering innovation, cultivating talent, and shaping institutions that are ready for the future. Whether guiding organizations in strategic transformation or engaging with students and professionals, he believes that education, when paired with purposeful leadership, has the power to drive significant and lasting change. With a deep appreciation for every experience and lesson along the way, Anish remains grounded in humility and gratitude. He values the power of positive words, encouragement, and the countless lessons shared with him throughout his journey. His story is a testament to the idea that genuine curiosity, integrity, and a forward-looking vision can inspire not only personal growth but also broader institutional excellence in a rapidly changing world.